Religion and Freedom of Thought

RELIGION
& Freedom of Thought

by

PERRY MILLER

ROBERT L. CALHOUN

NATHAN M. PUSEY

REINHOLD NIEBUHR

Foreword by Henry P. Van Dusen

Essay Index Reprint Series

 BOOKS FOR LIBRARIES PRESS
FREEPORT, NEW YORK

INTERNATIONAL STANDARD BOOK NUMBER:
0-8369-2199-2

LIBRARY OF CONGRESS CATALOG CARD NUMBER:
78-128296

PRINTED IN THE UNITED STATES OF AMERICA

Foreword

COLUMBIA UNIVERSITY is celebrating this year the bicentennial of its founding with a series of convocations, conferences, and other notable events, focusing upon the theme, "Man's Right to Knowledge and the Free Use Thereof."

Union Theological Seminary is not only one of Columbia's nearest neighbors on Morningside Heights, New York City. It is also linked to the University academically as one of the group of constituents which together make up this notably comprehensive educational institution. In the Columbia University system, Union Seminary serves, in effect, as its divinity school. Delegates from the Seminary faculty sit upon the University Council, discharging essentially the same rights and responsibilities as the representatives of Columbia College, Teachers College, Barnard, and the other units of the University. The Seminary also joins with the University in offering a variety of programs leading to masters' and doctors' degrees in the field of religion. On the other hand, Union Seminary is, administratively and financially, wholly independent. This rather unusual arrangement has linked the two institutions in happy and mutually fruitful association for more than a quarter of a century.

The Seminary faculty desired to pay tribute to Columbia University on the occasion of its anniversary and to make some small contribution to its deliberations. It seemed obvious that the most appropriate one might be an exploration of the meeting point of the bicentennial theme and the central concern of theological education: "Religion and Freedom of the Mind." If there is urgent contemporary relevance in the main theme, there is hardly less in this particular aspect of it. Historically, the relation of religion to intel-

5

lectual freedom has been a subject of heated debate. At the present time, when freedom of thought stands in jeopardy, the related query of whether religion, as a personal faith and as a social force, can be looked to as ally or foe, as an aid or an impediment, warrants special investigation. Hence, a one-day conference on "The Relation between Religion and Freedom of the Mind" was planned. One hundred and fifty scholars from thirteen universities and colleges and theological seminaries within the larger metropolitan area responded to the invitation to participate in its discussions. The addresses given in that connection furnish the material for this book.

The conference was planned and directed by Professor John C. Bennett of the Seminary, and Dr. Bennett has prepared this volume for the press.

HENRY P. VAN DUSEN *President*
Union Theological Seminary, New York City

CONTENTS

The Location of American Religious Freedom

PERRY MILLER

In JULY, 1849, George P. Putnam published a romance written by a doctor, one William Starbuck Mayo, weirdly entitled *Kaloolah*. For the firm, the book was a risk, since the story was, in substance, similar to a romance that had appeared earlier that year, written by Herman Melville and as weirdly entitled *Mardi*. Both works told of an adventurer's long quest for a mysterious white girl, Melville's amid the brown-skinned savages of Polynesia and Mayo's among the brown-skinned Bedouins of the Sahara. Two years before Melville had made a sensation with his supposedly autobiographical account of life among the cannibals. Mayo was accused of imitating him, especially as his book clearly had a somewhat autobiographical character. Mayo indignantly denied that he was copying Melville, though we may easily believe that he was. However that may be, the literary gods, or rather the public, were capricious. Melville's book was a dismal failure, while *Kaloolah* was a success, running rapidly through several editions. There was then no "bestseller list," but for months it would have topped any bookseller's report. Today *Kaloolah* is remembered, if at all, only for its analogies to Melville, but in 1849 it hit, as we might say, the jack-pot.

The youth of the hero is spent in an up-state New York town, which clearly is Ogdensburg, where Mayo was born in 1811. This part of the nation, I need hardly remind you, was known at the time as the "burned-over district," a region swept from end to end by a succession of religious revivals that culminated in the 1820s in the torrential whirlwind of Charles Grandison Finney, who introduced into the technique of whipping up zeal the ingenious device of praying for hardened sinners, or indeed for anybody who opposed the revival, by name in the church, giving a public catalogue of their offenses. *Kaloolah* relates that when this particular frenzy hit the hero's town, it brought to a halt not only all business but the local Academy, for students and faculty alike deserted classrooms to confess their sins and to pray with gusto over those of their fellows.

> *It spread itself like an epidemic, and seemed to be governed by similar laws. Rapidly increasing in violence as it advanced, it attacked all classes, but evinced particular power over the very young, the very aged and the very vicious. No revival in that section of country had ever been more complete, or had been more strongly characterized by enthusiastic zeal and intense, wild, passionate excitement.*

It emanated, Mayo significantly says, from all churches in the town—Baptist, Methodist, and Presbyterian—and engulfed virtually the whole population except the president of the Academy, who was also pastor of the Presbyterian church. He set himself stoutly "against what his good sense led him to pronounce an unhealthy, if not an unholy excitement," and for this resistance he paid heavily. "A highly cultivated mind, refined taste, gentle manner and undoubted piety served not to save him from contumely and insult." His own congregation insulted him by praying for him, with clear allusions "to age, situation, connections, and prospects." Our minds inevitably leap ahead to practices recently reported from countries we call "totalitarian" when Mayo says that small children were used to work upon or to denounce their parents, and that pretty girls were employed to lead adoring swains to the anxious seat.

Now I think there are two observations that must occur to any modern American who reads this description. One is the striking fact that in America of 1849 this terrifying episode could be presented as revolting only in a work of admittedly unrealistic fiction. Had Mayo made a full–dress, frontal attack on revivalism, his book would never have come anywhere near the best-seller list. We know that clergymen who did venture to attack revivals, not because they disapproved the end but because they disliked the methods, suffered even fouler abuse than Mayo's gentle Presbyterian in Ogdensburg. The student of religious periodicals of the 1840s finds things said, for instance, about Dr. John H. Nevin and his wonderfully sane book, *The Anxious Bench*, which he would hardly believe any professing Christian could utter about another, were it not that his incredulity has lately been dissipated by the spectacle of Boston's newspapers and some investigating committees of the Congress of the United States.

The second, and more obvious, reflection invited by this passage takes the form of a question: Where, in this land that then, as now, boasted it had for the first time in world history achieved complete religious liberty—where was the freedom?

As a matter of fact, Mayo proceeds to tell us precisely where it was. I dwell upon this prescription not because *Kaloolah* is another *Moby-Dick*, but precisely because it was popular in 1849 and was still popular in 1851 when the public ignored *Moby-Dick*. With the school disrupted, the hero fled to the woods. He went to Nature. He stretched himself upon a sunny bank or sat upon a prostrate giant of the forest; there he "turned with shuddering and loathing from the sight and sounds of the distant village," and found himself persuaded "that cant and rant are utterly inconsistent with the true worship of God." So, for several pages Mayo chants the religion of Nature with which his romance is suffused. "How soft, and low, and calm, yet deep and full of meaning and power are the hymns sung to His Praise in the great temple of Nature." And indeed, not only is Nature in repose preferable to the raucous tumult of a revival, but in its awful and destructive might it is more so, even in the tempest.

> *Stand forth, and enjoy it! Quail not! Bare your brow to the storm—look with a steady eye upon the lightning's flash—listen to the awful chorus and feel alike the infinity of God and the greatness of the soul.*

As a piece of prose, this bears no comparison with Captain Ahab's address to Nature's furious fire in the neglected book of 1851, but Melville's message is much the same:

> *Here again with haughty agony, I read my sire. Leap! leap up, and lick the sky. I leap with thee; I burn with thee; fain would be welded with thee; defyingly I worship thee!*

These two writers,—the lesser and popular one, the great neglected one—were not cloistered scholars; both had a large experience of American life. Both managed to say, through the indirections in which they were obliged to hide themselves, through romantic fictions, that freedom of the mind is not to be found in a sniveling church which humiliates a man by advertising his sins, but in the sublimity of Nature, even though that sublimity slay him.

Melville found in man's embrace of Nature a terror so Titanic that his masterpiece frightened his contemporaries; yet just because it does plunge so deeply it can be called the most profound reading of the American mentality achieved in its day, and its rediscovery in our own time is proof that its diagnosis remains valid. Certainly the cult of Nature became in the first half of the nineteenth century a conspicuous manifestation of the American mind. It can be found on all levels of culture, from the novels of Cooper, the poems of Bryant, the landscapes of the Hudson River School, down to the mawkish gift-books and annuals. It even flourished on the frontier, in the face of floods, forest-fires, the ague, and the camp meeting. As has often been remarked, Emerson's little book of 1836 is a central document for the epoch if only for its title, *Nature*. Though at first Emerson caused alarm by too cavalierly dispensing with the last pretense of a specifically Christian revelation, by proclaiming the utter sufficiency of Nature to supply the life of the spirit, yet by his own saintliness and by the eupeptic properties of his doctrine, he won an astonishing acceptance even among those church-goers who thought themselves impeccably orthodox. "Self-reliance" was just what a nation needed that had before it the enormous task of conquering a continent, and consistency could be happily scorned as an unnatural hobgoblin by busy men who no longer wanted to be checked by petty divines. In the second half of the century, Emerson along with Longfellow was quoted from innumerable American pulpits in order to clarify the more enigmatic utterances of the Gospels.

This cult of Nature had its vogue, we should remark, among the better educated, the sort of people who shared and who came increasingly to share Mayo's distaste for the antics of revivalism. One would hardly expect to find much of it among the leaping shouters, the yelping and jerking converts at the mammoth Cain Ridge meeting. Anyone who knows the New England peasantry—whom we never call peasants but always "natives"—knows that you can never get an authentic Vermont farmer to admire the view, but when the New Englander, even at evangelical Amherst, has risen in the cultural scale to that of Judge Dickinson, he will seize the rope and ring the church bell like mad to call the townspeople's attention to an especially gorgeous sunset.

Now we must always remember that this ubiquitous cult of Nature has its efflorescence just at the moment when this country—the first, as we have said, in world history to make the experiment—is feeling the full effects of realizing in a body politic the ideal of complete religious liberty. It had indeed become the proudest among all America's proud boasts, that here a man can worship as he chooses. Here is no established church, no tithe, no ecclesiastical court; here there is a wall of separation between state and church. Any group of persons can come together and form any kind of

church, believe in anything they fancy (except, of course, in polyg-
amy!), and as long as they obey the civil laws and do not get the notion
that religion means sharing the wealth of John Jacob Astor, they can go
their way unmolested. If this is not freedom of the mind, what in Heaven's
name is?

It was a problem for patriotic and liberal historians like George Bancroft
—whose *History*, by the way, is a major exhibit in the cult of Nature, for in it
natural guidance has finally and utterly replaced supernatural providence—
to explain just how Americans acquired their passionate devotion to the
principle of religious liberty. Scholars hesitated to give all, or even any, of
the credit to Thomas Jefferson, because while he had venerated nature, his
was the nature of the Newtonian scientist, not Nature spelled with capital
N, which Cooper celebrated, Thomas Cole painted, and to which Mayo's
hero fled for relief from the din of the revival. When they went back to the
pre-Revolutionary churches, especially those historians who were members
in good standing of one of the principal denominations, they had trouble
not only with the original, and "misguided," philosophies of their forbears,
but in discovering the reasons for the churches' conversion to what had now
become the realized American dream. Descendants of the Puritans inevitably had particular difficulty, for it was no easy task to convince themselves
that churches that had exiled Roger Williams and Anne Hutchinson, had
whipped Baptists and indubitably hanged Quakers, were prophets of the
First Amendment. Presbyterians and Anglicans were almost as embarrassed,
and while the record of the Baptists before the Revolution was good, still
they had been small and despised groups who clearly had advocated toleration in order to get out from under their oppressors. The Methodists had
come so late on the scene that they had no colonial past to plague them, but
no one quite had the temerity to present John Wesley as a pioneer of the
American conception of religious liberty. The history of colonial New York
was a puzzle beyond a puzzle, because there, where English rule had tried
to keep both the Dutch Reformed Church and the Church of England established, diversity of sects had come in such bewildering profusion that the
ultimate triumph of religious liberty seemed rather an exhausted and a
cynical resignation to the inevitable than any upsurge of positive conviction.
True, the Quakers could claim that from the beginning William Penn welcomed all Christians to his emporium. Bancroft, as a matter of fact, dared
to hold up Penn to admiration, in explicit contrast to his own maniacal ancestors, as one prematurely inspired by that spirit of Nature which, emanating
in Bancroft's day in the form of Kantian philosophy, had taught America

the categorical imperative of freedom. Still, the Quakers were only one, and a relatively small, group; nobody could seriously argue that the fathers of the Constitution and framers of state constitutions had arrived at the conclusion of religious liberty by studying Quaker precedents.

Actually, if for historians like Bancroft and Palfrey it was a bother to show exactly how the several denominations, starting with philosophies of exclusiveness and intolerance, had yet come in America to pride themselves on letting others live their own lives, for the historian of today, especially on such an occasion as this, it remains a vexation. For a long time there was a disposition, particularly among historians glorying in the name of liberalism, to search the American past in order to pick out and to laud the few figures who can be said to have pointed the way. Penn still receives unstinted praise, although I suspect that the terms employed in the lavish encomium might astonish and even dismay that benevolent autocrat. The most unfortunate obfuscation compounded by well-intentioned but historically inappropriate adoration has been that which buried in verbiage the majestic figure of Roger Williams. I have lately made a small effort to excavate him, and I must confess that, as notices of the book come to me from all over the country, I am amazed to see with what startled amazement reviewers greet the news that the founder of Providence was named Williams and not Thomas Jefferson. Perhaps even more mischievous has been the attempt of American historians and orators—a generation ago it might be said to have amounted to a conspiracy—to prove that somehow, in the very genes of the Protestant churches, and despite anything they may have said or done in the seventeenth century, the principle of liberty was latent. In this view, American history is seen as a steady translation into actuality of a potentiality inherent in the covenanted churches of Massachusetts, in Presbyterian synods of Philadelphia, in the vestries of Virginia, although neither New Englanders nor the Scotch-Irish nor even the genial planters of the Old Dominion had the slightest suspicion of its existence. If to this version of man proposing but God disposing, we can somehow add a conviction that the Almighty was especially conducting America by the hand of His Providence, we then manage to put ourselves into a happier relation with our ancestors, even though at the same time we have made them into a collection of libertarian Typhoid Marys, carrying unwittingly the germs of a contagion to which they themselves were immune.

To take a concrete example, loyal Harvard men are always seeking to unriddle how Harvard College, founded, at least so the founders said, in order that a literate ministry should continue in the churches after the pres-

ent ministers lay in the dust—which took its motto "Veritas" to mean not
an anthropologist's truth about marital rites in Timbuctoo or a physicist's
paradoxical truth about the propensity of certain esoteric materials toward
fission and toward fusion—but to mean simply and entirely "Christo et
Ecclesiae"—it is a riddle, I say, how from this theological acorn grew the
oak which today is in certain quarters reputed to be godless.

I think what happened with Harvard is, in slight measure, a help toward
comprehending what happened in America. Loyal Harvard men like to insist
that even under Puritan rule no loyalty oath was exacted from student or
teacher; but this is to ignore the fact that any member of the College who
then broached a heretical notion would have been immediately and sum-
marily disposed of by the civil arm. They endeavor also to extract from the
statement of the founders that, dreading to leave an illiterate ministry, they
intended "to advance learning and to perpetuate it to posterity," the welcome
conclusion that Harvard never was a mere "theological seminary." They forget that for these founders there was only one body of learning, the specified
and codified liberal arts, which constituted "learning," and that there was no
conceivable way this monolithic system could be subdivided, with some portion prescribed for secular students and the rest for theologians. Up to the
B.A. all pursued the same curriculum; if a few, and then progressively more,
left at that point, they merely stopped before coming to the queen of the
sciences, and so did not take an M.A. But that there was any question of
Harvard's being or not being a theological seminary was utterly unimagin-
able to the founders.

Without going into the long story of how history operated, it is enough
to say that with the increase of knowledge, of new arts and sciences, and
with the breaking-up of the old into "departments," and above all, with the
demand made upon Harvard and then upon all colleges to send men into
professions and into business, the unpredictable and unforeseeable thing
happened: the Divinity School became a graduate school, along with Den-
tistry, Forestry and (though not at Harvard) Hotel Management. It became
a mystery for specialists, not required of ordinary students; it became a
peculiarity in which one might indulge if he liked or wanted to earn a living
(a modest one) that way. Thus was freedom of the mind achieved at Harvard University.

The point is, to put it baldly, that both in education and in religion, we
didn't aspire to freedom, we didn't march steadily toward it, we didn't
unfold the inevitable propulsion of our hidden nature: we stumbled into it.
We got a variety of sects as we got a college catalogue: the denominations

and the sciences multiplied until there was nothing anybody could do about them. Wherefore we gave them permission to exist, and called the result freedom of the mind. Then we found, to our vast delight, that by thus negatively surrendering we could congratulate ourselves on a positive and heroic victory. So we stuck the feather in our cap and called it Yankee Doodle. Revivalists, whether in Mayo's Ogdensburg or in Gopher Prairie, or more genteel ones in Westchester County, have always been enthusiastic celebrants of our God-given religious liberty. I think it was Mr. Justice Holmes who remarked that in the Boston of his boyhood, you could safely deny the divinity of Christ but you would be overwhelmed with the utmost social opprobrium if you advocated sports on Sunday.

But to come back to the cult of Nature; the period when it throve was that which witnessed the dramatic—we might say the melodramatic—working out of America's discovery that the freedom of the Christian man can be boiled down from the abstruse speculations of Augustine, Aquinas, Luther, Calvin, Edwards, to one simple and practical *modus vivendi,* which consists of letting everybody do what he likes. One might say of the Protestant churches up to and through the Civil War that they, too, were built as Hosea Bigelow said the Confederacy was

> *on our bran-new politickle thesis*
> *That a Gov'ments fust right is to tumble to pieces.*

Protestantism may carry in its loins the dissidence of dissent, but even a Bossuet would be hard put to chronicle and keep straight the splinterings, separations, schisms, broils and divorces which constitute American church history from 1776 to 1865. I shall not inflict upon you the story of Unitarianism and then Transcendentalism out of Unitarianism; of Bellamyites and Hopkinsians, New Lights and Old, and the explosive New Haven Theology; of the Cumberland Presbytery, the Missouri Synod, the trial of Lyman Beecher, the Disciples of Christ, the Millerites, and the Christian Adventists. I sometimes try to put on the blackboard for my students a chart of the fragmentation of the churches in these years, and I end up with something as labyrinthine as the genealogies of York and Lancaster, amid which even Shakespeare got confused. When you add to this maze the severances of the Civil War, you begin to understand why so many conscientious and Christian persons, why, indeed, so many of the clergy themselves, without (as they supposed) abandoning Christian belief, turned to the enduring, the consoling, the uncontentious verities of Nature. They all read Wordsworth, and he told them what they wanted to hear:

One impulse from a vernal wood
May teach you more of man,
Of moral evil and of good
Than all the sages can.

Surely there was no harm in thus exercising a Christian's freedom? Emerson might, for some queer Yankee reason, feel obliged, once he turned to the vernal wood, to get out of the church, but Wordsworth never did. And besides, even Emerson so expounded the new doctrine that a true believer could delight in it:

Therefore is nature glorious with form, color, and motion, that every globe in the remotest heaven; every chemical change from the rudest crystal up to the laws of life; every change of vegetation from the first principle of growth in the eye of a leaf, to the tropical forest and antediluvian coal-mine; every animal function from the sponge up to Hercules, shall hint or thunder to man the laws of right and wrong, and echo the Ten Commandments.

I am proposing a thesis which you may think too ingenious, but which I believe is not quite fantastic. Take the first decades of this Republic as your testing ground—as a matter of fact, you can also take subsequent ones— and you will find that you must locate the tension between religion and freedom of the mind not amid the multitudinous jarring sects but between two definable extremes. On the one hand, there is a Biblicist and ineradicably revivalistic piety, saying with Thomas Campbell, "Where the Scriptures speak, we speak; where the Scriptures are silent, we are silent." On the other, there is a naturalism more or less spiritualized, becoming if anything more appealing to large numbers of Americans when, with the help of Darwin, Nature was found not so much to thunder the Ten Commandments as positively to yodel the Gospel of Wealth.

This dichotomy does become clear when we place in opposition Emerson and such infatuated revivalists as Peter Cartwright and Alexander Campbell. These exhorters were so intent upon working cataclysmic conversions—as Abraham Lincoln said, "When I hear a man preach, I like to see him fight bees"—that they were impervious to the forces even then sweeping their communities into Emersonian complacency. They were handicapped when confronting the new conceptions not only by their Biblicism but even more by their axiomatic retention of the empirical psychology of John Locke, by that sensationalism upon which Edwards had established the theory of revivalism, but which had become with them, as it had not been with him, mechanical. They may have read Byron and Scott, because everybody did, but they could not cope with Schleiermacher, Coleridge or Newman. Here, I would contend, is the beginning of the division which later in the century became the fatal cleavage between what, for short-hand purposes, we may call Fundamentalism and all the many forms of liberalism that found support for a genteel theism in evolution and in the "Higher Criticism." The line of battle was not so clear in 1850 as in 1900 only because the revivalists were still too busy fighting bees while the naturalists were still too vague or too little interested in ideas to lay down an open defiance of the dominant orthodoxy. Those who did perceive the dreadful rift—the most perceptive being Herman Melville—masked their dread in allegories uncomprehended by their contemporaries.

Fruitful analysis of the situation would be infinitely easier if only the mass of these innocent worshipers—one often wants to call them idolaters—of Nature had not all the time professed to be good Christians. Low-brows and high-brows alike read Byron and Scott. The drowning of Catherine Beecher's fiancé in 1822 brought his library to her house; Lyman prohibited his children from touching the books until he had veted them, but he delighted the family by reporting: "You may read Scott's novels. I have always disapproved of novels as trash, but in these is real genius and real culture, and you may read them." Outside Concord, Massachusetts, those who embraced Wordsworth and Coleridge insisted that the new philosophy was authentic Christianity. The Rev. Caleb S. Henry, an Episcopalian but a student of German, strove valiantly in the only journal of the time which can be said intellectually to rival *The Dial*, *The New York Review*, to show that Coleridge was no transcendentalist in the Emersonian sense, "denying or refining away the historic truth of Christianity." The *Review* said that Emerson's writings, purporting to be ambrosial food, were in reality poison; in this pantheistic perversion of Coleridge it found a striking instance of the inherent lawlessness of the American mind—"the evil and punishment of our age and country." Yet this same *Review*, in less guarded pages, is full of hymns to Nature; it too forgets repeatedly that the Christian should admire in Nature only the handiwork of God, and treats the landscape as a self-sufficient source of morality and law.

There were only a few who perceived the problem and attempted to mediate between extremes. I think we ought so to interpret the Mercersburg theology of Nevin and Schaff, but the man preëminently the hero and the victim of the predicament is Horace Bushnell. I am at a loss to comprehend why students of divinity in this nation are so ignorant of him; a few years ago Dean Weigle brought out through the Yale University Press an edition of Bushnell's *Christian Nurture* of 1847, but University Presses, though commendably eager to print good books, are universally averse from stooping to anything so vulgar as selling them, and Dean Weigle's edition seems not to have been widely noted. However, one must say that Bushnell, along with his magnificent restatement of the Atonement and the Trinity, also preached a kind of racist imperialism—what he called the "out-populating principle"—that makes him repugnant to those who today would hold to a complete freedom of the mind.

We are thus obliged to seek further into the reason why the cult of Nature made, and still makes, so tremendous an appeal to Americans. In the "romantic era" all Western Culture found new charms in Nature, but there is something decidedly different between the appeal of Nature in Germany and in Paris and that which it developed in America. Actually, the reason is not far to seek. Nature assuaged persons like Mayo who were disgusted with a narrow and noisy revivalism, but more importantly it gave Americans a rationale for America. To take one example out of millions: in 1835 James Brooks, later editor of *The New York Express,* published in *The Knickerbocker Magazine* a series entitled "Our Own Country," which made a great stir and was reprinted across the country. America does unfortunately show a preference for things material over the mental and spiritual, said Brooks, but we should not despair: the time is coming when we shall wax great in culture. And how may we be certain of this? Because God Himself has told us. And how has God spoken?

> *God speaks this promise in the sublimity of Nature. It resounds all along the crags of the Alleghanies. It is uttered in the thunder of Niagara. It is heard in the roar of two oceans, from the great Pacific to the rocky ramparts of the Bay of Fundy. His finger has written it in the broad expanse of our inland seas, and traced it out by the mighty Father of Waters. The august* TEMPLE *in which we dwell was built for lofty purposes. Oh! that we may consecrate it to* LIBERTY *and* CONCORD, *and be found fit worshippers within its holy walls.*

Nature therefore is not only God rebuking the hysteria of Charles Grandison Finney, it is the American TEMPLE. It means primarily freedom for the nation, only incidentally freedom for the mind. Concessions could be made to historic Christian doctrines, lip-service paid to Original Sin, and occasional worries expressed about American lawlessness; yet in the exhilarating vision of the panoramic TEMPLE the last vestiges of Christian pessimism could be exorcised (except by a Hawthorne, or by a Melville who, in the full tide of irony, said of himself, "I was a good Christian; born and bred in the bosom of the infallible Presbyterian church"). I supposed when I was writing the second volume of *The New England Mind* that I was slyly exposing the temptations that beset, in modern times, prophets who, taking themselves for Isaiahs and Jeremiahs, try to pass judgment upon a social process in which they are inextricably involved. But an astute friend said he found the book a case-history of "what happens to God in America." Perhaps he was only putting into more precise language what I had imagined I was saying.

It *is* a hard conundrum, isn't it? this liberty of the Christian man. It is tricky even in the exquisite analyses of Thomas Aquinas. In Protestantism it has always had to take the form of paradox. As Luther put it, the Christian is master of all, the Christian is servant of all. Our straightforward America has never been comfortable in the presence of paradox, refuses to allow that in our history there has been any trace of it, and becomes enraged when confronted with antinomy. Some may remember the dismay Reinhold Niebuhr spread when he propounded the paradox of moral man and immoral society. I know a clergyman who snarled at me that Niebuhr was ridiculing virtue and apologizing for sin. I remember thinking, but *not* saying, that if we take the word "apologia" in its highest sense, is not "apologia for sin," come to think of it, a fair working definition of Christianity?

The paradox is so hazardous to live with that men constantly seek a more plausible, a less torturing, freedom at one or the other of its extremities. The first we might call Quietism, if we may stretch the term to include unquiet revivalism: it says, "I am master by letting the all overwhelm me. I remain free amid persecutions, tempests, and the incessant bombardment of advertisers because I keep my Christian liberty safe and snug inside me, knowing that despite persecutors and singing commercials on television, I shall be gloriously free beyond the grave." The second way we may call activism: I throw the function of servitude upon the Atonement so that, secure in the knowledge that it has been vicariously done for me, I plunge into action—the action to which I am invited by Nature. Thus I settle the continent, free the slaves, get votes for women, buy the advertised toothpaste, and so become a citizen in the most powerful nation on earth, all the time singing ecstatic hymns to the nation's holy walls and calling myself free. Surely *this* is freedom? It is even *more* than freedom: it is the American Way of Life.

Yet there does seem, somehow, an inadequacy in both these common-sensical resolutions of the paradox. There appears to be a mysterious, an ominous, complementary quality about the two, as though they belong together even while they contradict each other. As my wise father-in-law said when his small daughter asked what is the difference between Unitarians and Universalists, "The Unitarians don't believe in Heaven, the Universalists don't believe in Hell." And in some strange fashion, the consequence of both seems to be that all responsibility is taken off the self and put upon the group. If "they" hurl the hydrogen bomb at us, I am obliged to insist it is none of my doing, "they" did it. But if "we" throw it first at them, I still am not to blame, for "we" did it. When the child spills the ink and is scolded, he says "I didn't do it, it did its own self." I who live amid holy walls am my own master, am I not? To this sorry and desperate pass, I sometimes think, has the popular conception of freedom sunk in this our nominally Christian culture.

As many have noticed, the Protestant Churches in America, even though brought from Europe, show more qualities in common than any one retains with its European stem. And they feel that in America the synagogue is no longer an alien. Even the Catholic Church in America acquires a tone unlike Catholicism in Europe. All have grown and prospered within these holy walls. But a horrible thought keeps intruding itself: have these bodies displayed on this magnificent continent the spirit of freedom, have they fostered it, can the churches take *any* credit for it? Or have they not become, and have they not in truth always been, groups of interest, class, race or consanguinity, elements in an evolution which is to be explained not from within but from without, not by the spirit of Christ but by the natural environment, not by the paradox but by economic and geographic circumstances. The two powers whom we had supposed contending for the allegiance of America, both chanting the slogan of freedom—both the Bible and Nature turn out to have been hand-in-glove behind the scene. Both, in the end, become sanctifiers not of freedom but of conformity. They unite in order to condemn what is "un-American."

I need not remind an audience in Union Theological Seminary that the Christian conscience of the Republic has not been entirely silent before this enormity. Nor has the Christian intelligence proved so obtuse as to be wholly fooled. I have mentioned Niebuhr. I have lately witnessed the intense delight with which students come to the ending of Paul Tillich's *The Courage to Be*: when they read his declaration that we must seek the God behind the God, they rejoice in the exercise of a freedom which in essence is that liberation from what the Germans call (or used to call) "Philisterhaft," that emancipation we most devoutly pray for.

The universities and churches of Germany, we know, have been put to a hard school to learn the lesson of freedom. I like to think that in the darkest of their days some of them might have remembered the University of Jena on November 7, 1825. That was the day on which Duke Karl-August of Saxe-Weimar held a civic celebration of the fiftieth anniversary of Goethe's coming to court. No doubt the University was disposed to please its patron, but its performance on this grandiose occasion was not obsequious. The Faculties of Philosophy and Medicine bestowed honorary degrees of Doctor; the Faculty of Law would have voted Goethe one did he not already have a Doctorate from Strasbourg—this being a naïve time it was thought that one degree of each kind, even honorary, was enough! But the Faculty of Theology was in a bit of a quandary: somehow a Doctorate of Theology did not seem quite appropriate for Goethe. So they resolved to give him instead an inscribed diploma, which Goethe prized above all the gifts he received on that bountiful day. They said:

> *Your Excellency has not only often elevated our peculiar branch of knowledge, and the principles on which it rests, by profound, enlightened, and awakening remarks, but, as creator of a new spirit in science and in life, and as lord of the domain of free and vigorous thought, has powerfully promoted the true interests of the church and of evangelical theology.*

The vexed problem of religion and freedom of the mind might be immensely clarified if and when it can be stoutly declared in this country that the Faculty's statement is profoundly religious.

The pattern of American life and the clearly prefigured destiny of America seemed to the founders and to virtually all Americans for over a century thereafter to be the final simplification of history: liberty and concord within the holy walls of Nature. But the Christian insight has always discerned, even though dimly, that freedom is not a simple business. American society has moved from simplicity to complexity, even assuming that the early communities were actually as simple as we imagine. By its very paradoxicality, the Christian concept of freedom thrusts into the heart of the nation's struggle with itself a dimension which the nation might be happier, or at least more comfortable, could it be disregarded. The natural response is to cry, "Let us alone; what have we to do with thee? We're doing all right, aren't we?" But if the paradox perpetually causes self-dissatisfaction, it also imparts a curious glory; it has, even in this most prosperous of nations, thwarted our complacency, filled us with unrest, disturbed our sleep and permitted us no peace of mind. It has constantly made us ask whether we really are doing all right. If the enigma of Christian liberty, the conundrum of the freedom of the religious mind, has remained obstinately insoluble, we may gratefully acknowledge that it will as surely continue to be stubbornly recalcitrant.

The Historical Relations between
Religion and Intellectual Freedom

ROBERT L. CALHOUN

DURING THE CENTURY and a quarter between the outbreak of the
French Revolution and the beginning of World War I, there was a general
and growing conviction in the Western world that religion—especially organized, institutional, dogmatic religion—is fundamentally incompatible with intellectual freedom. During that time, it would have been granted by most
enlightened observers in the West that there can be a mild, cerebral kind
of piety, of the innocuous sort described in Hume's *Dialogues,* that need
not interfere with free inquiry. But it was rather generally agreed among
both church members and their critics that full-blooded, vigorous religion,
usually presumed to be authoritarian, is necessarily unfriendly to freedom
of thought.

In the time since 1917, when both organized Christianity and secular
life have been undergoing revolutionary changes and anxious restudy, this
easy rationalistic assumption is proving far too simple. Within the past forty
years, we have found ourselves involved once more in the sort of paradoxical
situation that existed when the early Christian martyrs confronted the pagan
empire, when monks and clergy of the ninth century defended the freedom
of the Christian Church and gospel against the barbarian princes of western
Europe, or when the Puritans, Covenanters, and Independents of the English
and Scottish Reformation refused to give way before Tudor and Stuart autoc-
racy. In such a time, lines are not neatly drawn. Among the sturdiest de-
fenders of freedom, including freedom of conscience and of thought, are
likely to be many who must seem to any rationalist the very models of

intolerance and obscurantism, and who in fact might well on occasion be repressive and dictatorial toward those who seemed to them to be enemies of the truth. We are dealing here not merely with the familiar fact that human motives are always mixed, and often full of inconsistency. When we talk of religion and of intellectual freedom, we are talking about the very marrow of human existence that is far too fluid and full of ambiguity to be analyzed into simple factors. Both intellectual freedom and religion, because both are rooted in the core of man's being, show this sort of stubborn ambivalence both in value and in descriptive character. That is one reason that the problems they pose for us are at once of vital urgency and incapable of being once for all resolved.

Any brief discussion of these problems must obviously be arbitrary and incomplete. I suggest that we try here to see them in two main perspectives. The first is normative: the effort to recognize some of the major values and disvalues that intellectual freedom and religious commitment involve for human well-being. The second is descriptive or factual: concern to examine the relations that have existed in fact, and that exist in principle between religion and freedom of thought. We shall give attention here chiefly to the task of determining what relations exist in fact and in principle. But it seems well to begin with a brief consideration of the values and disvalues involved on both sides.

I. *Significance of Intellectual Freedom and Religious Commitment for Human Well-being*

When we speak here of intellectual freedom, we have in view the opportunity for unimpeded inquiry and communication, in pursuit of better understanding of man and the universe. The capacity for pursuit of such understanding and the demand for such opportunity are rooted in the nature of man.

They have easily recognizable roots in the familiar impulses of curiosity and sociability. Man like his nearest kinsmen among the primates displays an all but irrepressible urge to explore whatever comes within the range of his experience. In large part, this curiosity is pragmatic and utilitarian, directed to solving immediate practical problems, and so achieving desired comforts or overcoming present frustrations. But among men, at least, this pragmatic curiosity develops another dimension: a more or less purely theoretic impulse simply to discover what is the case. The special satisfaction sought at this level is not the gratifying of a desire for food or some other ulterior end, but the satisfaction of the very impulse to know. Practical effort seeks to change the existing state of affairs in some way, to make it accord better with the individual's desires or acknowledged obligations. Theoretic effort seeks rather not to change the situation but to see it more clearly as it is. At this level, the most distressing sort of frustration is likely to be the defeat of this craving for clear vision.

Inextricably bound up with human curiosity is the impulse to seek the company and sympathy of one's fellows. Whether we call this impulse sociability or something else, there is no doubt of its vital place in human life. It leads directly to efforts to exchange signals, to compare experiences, and in general to communicate what one has learned, partly in the hope of learning more. The more complex and subtle a man's experience becomes, the greater the need for communication with fellow-explorers, for the sake of correction and cross-fertilization of insights. The demand for intellectual freedom, then, the driving force that prompts men to seek it and prize it within whatever range of experience they know, is not a contrived or superficial whim. It is the force of deep-seated impulses that normally are strong and insistent, though doubtless subject to distortion and perhaps to virtual obliteration.

But man's capacity for such freedom lies even deeper. The primary roots of his need for intellectual freedom lie in the fundamental fact that he actually is free—as observer, inquirer, critic of his environment and of himself. Bound and limited though he is in the midst of his sustaining world, every human person is able to stand over against that world, to judge it and to reorder it in thought by comparing what is before him with what he remembers, or anticipates, or regards as possible and perhaps desirable. If a man were as completely contained in the present as a stone or a tree appears to be, it is inconceivable that he would be able thus to extricate himself from his immediate situation—even from the network of his own present impulses—so as to move in thought between present and past or future, between actuality and what is possible or valuable, better or worse. If this sort of freedom to think were removed from a human being, he would forthwith become as a tree or a mollusk and no longer a human being at all. Moreover, not only is a man thus incorrigibly free to think. He is capable also of accompanying thought with intelligent action, directed to the revision of his environment or of his own behavior patterns. The demand for intellectual freedom, therefore, is not merely a demand that strong human impulses shall attain satisfaction. It is even more fundamentally a demand that artificial restraint of one sort or another shall not be permitted to contradict the primary reality of human existence.

To say this is to indicate at once the vital values that are involved. Sufficient scope for critical inquiry and communication is indispensable for normal functioning and growth of human persons. Moreover, the need for such freedom is greater, not less, as persons become masters of more extensive and complex ranges of experience. Whatever rigidities and distortions of character within a man, and whatever political, social, or ecclesiastical pressures from without may prevent him from thinking and speaking freely will so far be impeding his normal growth as human being.

At the same time, it is necessary to recognize frankly the risks involved in the free play of human intelligence. There is, of course, a familiar and never-ending array of hazards that result from the products of human thought: the tools and weapons, the strategies and systems that continue to threaten human welfare in ever new and unanticipated ways. More fundamental risks, however, lie not merely in some of the results of thought, but in some ways of thinking. More and more, as our understanding of the world and ourselves has advanced, specialization has become indispensable; and specialization has tended very often to fragmentation and dangerous unbalance in our growing knowledge. This is in part the source of the fears that now confront us in a time of technological precocity and widespread moral illiteracy. Moreover, the uninhibited pursuit of knowledge all too frequently tends to isolate itself from the full concrete fabric of human concerns, and intellectual freedom is confused with social irresponsibility. These are risks that have to be taken if we are to continue to grow toward human maturity, and any arbitrary attempt to forestall them by repression is self-defeating. At the same time, they are risks that must not be ignored or minimized, and unceasing effort is needed to insure that growing freedom shall be practiced with growing maturity and responsibility.

In the actual course of human living, a powerful corrective to fragmentation and excessive detachment of the intellectual enterprise has been provided by religious conviction and commitment. This, too, has roots in natural impulses and in the natural existence of man. Its proximate roots are to be found, most obviously, in human tendencies that have much in common with those from which intellectual effort springs. Among these are, on the one hand, the impulses of wonder and repentance. The former, from which Aristotle derives the whole career of Greek philosophy, is closely related to curiosity in its purely theoretic form—the desire to see and know more clearly; but in wonder this theoretic impulse has added dimensions of admiration and awe in the presence of what is disclosed to the wondering mind. Repentance likewise is closely allied to this experience of vision, for it involves self-criticism and self-abasement in the presence of the Other that is revealed. Along with these tendencies goes a related craving for access to reality and for reconciliation with it. Again there is a reminder of one of the deep impulses underlying intellectual effort: the impulse we have called sociability, that seeks companionship and participation in a larger whole. But whereas before we were speaking of man's desire for the company and understanding of his fellows, we are speaking now of his desire for access to and acceptance by whatever is most ultimate in his world. The distinctive religious response is worship, in which these impulses and many more find complex expression.

But again, as in the case of intellectual effort, religious conviction is rooted beneath all conscious impulses in the very existence of man. For man as we know him is at once dependent upon the reality that gives him birth and sustains him, and obligated in a variety of ways to acknowledge and respond to its demands. This is a part of what Christian tradition has meant by saying that man is created according to the image of God. In his very existence, man is not self-sufficient but sustained by whatever Being is greatest and deepest in his world—or rather, he is dependent upon a Being too great and too high to be included within the limits of his world, the Ground of the world's existence also. In that dependence, the religious man recognizes obligation that gives character and substance to his life. In worship, not some portion of him but his whole existence is involved.

The vital values of such religious conviction for human life include, along with many others, a perpetual stimulation to realism about oneself and about the basis of one's dependent life, and therefore to a sense of proportion in both thought and action. The genuinely religious man will not think of himself more highly than his dependent status deserves. At the same time, he will find in his confrontation by the God whom he worships a fundamental validation of his own being, of the life of the communities of which he is a member, and, at least in principle, of the intellectual enterprise as quest for truth. The man who finds his ultimate ground and good in God, rather than in any earthly power, has a kind of freedom and fundamental confidence that can be had on no other terms.

But again, it is necessary to recognize the risks and distortions that are peculiar to the religious attitude. Among these, the most widespread and destructive is likely to be idolatry in some form. Whenever a man or a people finds the ultimate ground of confidence and obligation in something less than the God high above everything in nature and in human affairs—deifying a ruler, a people, or a political or ecclesiastical institution—idol-worship takes the place of high religion. The result is to inhibit human growth and often enough to distort human obligation, with the frightful results that have become all too familiar in our time. Another familiar pitfall of religion, not unrelated to its powerful driving energy, is impatience with critical inquiry, and the encouragement of obscurantism and anti-intellectual irresponsibility. Some of the unhappy consequences of this tendency we shall examine in a moment. For the present, it is perhaps enough to say that the distortions of both intellectual freedom and religious conviction can best be controlled when the two are kept in close and vigorous association.

II. *Interrelations of Organized Religion and Intellectual Inquiry in the West*

To offer this suggestion obviously poses at once the question whether in point of fact organized religion and systematic intellectual effort have been able to live in harmony. We shall concern ourselves primarily with the interrelations of institutional religion and the more systematic forms of theoretical inquiry—the sciences, scholarship, and philosophy—in the Western world. The common purpose of these familiar forms of theoretical inquiry is not primarily to change the existing state of affairs, but to attain understanding at once more comprehensive and more clear.

When we speak here of institutional religion, we have in mind, of course, the socialized expression of the religious impulse in cult, systematic proclamation and tradition both oral and written, and the more or less massive and enduring organization and discipline of a continuing religious community. Plainly enough, other factors than the primary components of religious response are involved here—factors that are determined largely by the nature of human society, and the particular culture, simple or complex, that is characteristic of a particular time and place. After reminding ourselves of some of the familiar influences of such organized or institutional religion upon the theoretic disciplines, we shall have to turn back finally to inquire about the more intrinsic relations that in principle exist as between religious conviction and intellectual freedom.

The three types of systematic theoretical inquiry here examined are no doubt sufficiently familiar to need little definition. But there may be some point in noticing briefly their distinctive characters and the conditions required for their effective development.

The sciences are most specialized and diverse in both subject matter and procedures. Each of them seeks to explore a selected segment of natural or cultural phenomena which promises to yield to more or less exact description and formulation, especially sensible phenomena to which the techniques of counting and measurement can be more or less directly applied. Their objectives when clearly understood are always limited in scope, and their results are abstract and schematic rather than fully concrete. No mature and clear-headed scientist would think of taking the universe as his field of inquiry. He narrows his sights quite deliberately upon some restricted, observable segment of what is open to his inspection, and has as his ideal a highly simplified, dispassionate, coherent summary of what can be observed or directly inferred therefrom. His concern as scientist is not to provide ultimate explanations, nor to cover the whole range of legitimate human knowledge. As a matter of fact, new sciences are constantly arising to carry forward more and more detailed inquiries with respect to observable areas that existing disciplines do not, perhaps cannot, sufficiently describe.

The sciences, more than scholarship and philosophy, often lend themselves more or less directly to practical or technological application; but their primary intent, in their purest and most distinctive forms, is to get more knowledge without regard to its immediate utility. A constant pressure for immediate practical results can distort or even cripple scientific inquiry. The sciences, moreover, lend themselves especially well to organized cooperative effort, with teams of specialists combining their inquiries in a joint attack on some complex problem. At times, this sort of organization of scientific inquiry can be carried out largely by routine workers whose contributions are comparable to those of skilled mechanics or calculating machines. Given suitable direction by a few highly expert and resourceful directors of research, and sufficient care in the use of established techniques by their subordinates, very great advances can be made by pooling the results of a great number of very modest efforts. This is the aspect of scientific work that makes it possible for highly competent inquiries to be carried out under rigid systems of control, and that lends frightening plausibility to such caricatures as *Brave New World* and *1984*. But it remains true that regimentation of scientific inquiry is sure to stunt and distort, if not to stifle its continuing growth, whenever it prevents the continual emergence of original minds capable of defining new problem areas and proposing new methods of attack. For the development of such minds, intellectual freedom from extraneous control is indispensable.

Scholarship comes into play at a somewhat different level. Scientific work requires the use of systems of symbols, verbal, numerical, and other, and of elaborate cumulative records as tools for its work. But symbols and records are used also for other than scientific purposes: to commemorate notable persons and events, to chronicle sequences of individual and human experience, to give expression to insights, feelings, and value judgments of many kinds. When such records and symbols themselves pose problems and become subject matter for investigation, scholars take their places beside the scientists as seekers after knowledge. Thus, languages fall out of current use and become dead languages, needing to be interpreted or perhaps to be wholly relearned. Inscriptions, books, libraries are damaged or destroyed, leaving gaps to be filled and fragments to be pieced together. Discrepancies appear in the record, puzzling allusions, mingled relics of diverse cultural strata, and conflicting reports of the same event that need to be put straight. Hence scholarship. The line between this sort of inquiry and the special sciences cannot and need not be rigidly drawn. History, for example, would claim both titles. Certainly it is no longer satisfactory, though not without suggestiveness, to say that the interests of the sciences are mainly naturalistic, those of scholarship mainly humanistic. In any event, the basic concern of both, in their most distinctive forms, is to get a clear understanding of facts and their interrelations, undistracted by concern for immediate practical use.

Philosophy, again, has much in common with both these other disciplines. It takes over large masses of data and numerous interpretative suggestions from both, and seeks by persistent reflection to work and rework them into coherent diagrams of reality more comprehensive, and therefore necessarily more speculative, than those at which any one of the special sciences or scholarly disciplines may arrive. To offset these borrowings, it has in turn contributed numerous special hypotheses to both, besides sharing with them the universal language of logic which philosophers have done much to devise and refine. And like them, it is primarily concerned to see more and more clearly the world as it is and may be. The common end of all these forms of theoretical inquiry, in short, is not immediate usefulness more insight whether immediately useful or not.

It is evident that all such enterprises require rather special favoring conditions for success. Besides the obvious need for wide varieties of data, both diverse and orderly, there must be suitable places and equipment for study: in especial, facilities for accumulating, preserving, distributing, and using records, without which cumulative work can hardly be done. There must, of course, be observers competent and favorably situated to conduct such inquiries. They must be secure and free, if they are to do their specialized jobs properly, not only in the way that all men need to be free if they are to learn and grow to full stature, but in various special ways as well.

They must be free in substantial measure from preoccupation with economic needs. They must have leisure, and the opportunity for long periods of study and training that may have little or no immediate utilitarian value. They must have opportunity for free association with other persons like themselves, interested in and competent for theoretical inquiry. For cross-fertilization of thought, and consequent multiplication and mutual improvement of ideas, contacts between observers of diverse training and cultural background is required. And it goes without saying that freedom from arbitrary social restraint upon the seeking or announcing of results is imperative for rapid advance.

At the same time, these special freedoms and immunities for intellectual workers are not to be thought of as arbitrary privileges that set them apart from their fellows, and insulate them from responsibility for the practical life of mankind. We have seen that a tendency to such insulation and irresponsibility is a distortion of the intellectual life rather than a proper characteristic of it. The disinterested quest for knowledge has its roots inescapably in the practical business of living, to which on the whole and in the long run it can and should contribute. The motives for such inquiry, as actually conducted by human beings, are necessarily mixed motives, among which transparent zeal for knowledge is but one. In the earlier stages of the development of intellectual enterprise, indeed, practical motives play the dominant role, and contribute indispensably to the rise of the intellectual life. The correlation is never a simple one, and practical concerns, as already noted, can distort and hamper as well as help the pursuit of knowledge.

On any view, systematic theoretical inquiry has in fact arisen and developed in the midst of cultures permeated by various forms of organized religion, which is far older than the sciences and philosophy; but whether such development has come about chiefly because of or in spite of the influence of religion is still a moot question. There is much evidence in support of either answer. Religion, in fact, has appeared at times as fostering parent or stanch ally, at times as repressive parent or jealous rival of the intellectual life. At times, no doubt, the relation between them has been cooler, a mutual tolerance more or less amicable; but dispassion is not characteristic of robust religion, and our concern here is mainly with religion as positive influence, not as aloof onlooker.

In what ways then has religion definitely influenced theoretical inquiry? Especially in their beginnings, but in varying degrees throughout their careers, the intellectual disciplines must depend upon the conjunction of various practical interests that are favorable, for the most part perhaps indirectly, to the rise of non-practical pursuits. Among the enterprises that embody such interests, organized religion has always held a conspicuous place. It has helped to provide suitable places, materials, and equipment for study; and it has helped to fit persons for theoretical work.

It was characteristic of religion in its earlier forms to single out certain places as sacred, protected from sacrilege by the superhuman power of daemons or gods. When to the natural inaccessibility of many such spots—caverns, hill-tops or high places, cliffs, ravines—were added reinforcements of heavy masonry in the form of tombs, temples, and palaces, it is not strange that these places often became favored repositories for precious objects, appropriate sites for wall paintings, inscriptions, and sculptures, and places for the production and preservation of literary records. To many of these objects and records themselves the character of sacredness attached, and their preservation and care was a religious duty. Together they formed the backbones of growing traditions. The venerable and often cryptic character of their older strata invited reflection, and rewarded it with the sense of participation in momentous knowledge. The well-guarded precincts in which they rested, moreover, were often places especially favorable for quiet study. And the net result was a long and close connection between religious sites and traditionalistic learning.

When, further, the old temples and shrines were supplemented as in post-exilic Judaism and Christianity, by synagogues, churches, and monasteries—places for congregational worship and for education as well as for ritual observance—the same connection was fostered in new settings and with new emphases. Recognition accorded to sacred places and care for sacred objects as such was continued. But an important body of religious opinion had now begun to hold that places and things were secondary; that the spoken will of God as announced in the sacred writings and interpreted to the people by authorized ministers and teachers was of greater importance. Learning now was no longer merely a secluded adjunct of religious folkways, a mysterious privilege of the few but no concern of the many. It came to be recognized as an essential factor in the development of the common religious life. Not all could be learned, but the wisdom of the learned was seen now as a heritage to be shared in some measure by humble laymen. Hence, in part, the impressive growth of systematic education under Jewish and Christian auspices.

But in proceeding thus far, we have already turned from places and things to persons. Just as ancient religion marked certain places for special immunity and significance, so it set apart certain persons—shamans, priests, prophets, kings—for special duties, immunities, and privileges. That some of these, at least, were persons of unusual nervous and mental organization is plain. They represented as a group, we may suppose, a higher average of variability in behavior—perhaps greater sensitiveness to impressions, certainly greater variety in response—than the mass of their fellows engaged in routine work. From this last they were more or less wholly freed. They had leisure not accorded to ordinary folk. They had access to whatever treasures, traditions, and records the group had accumulated. They had the advantages of co-operative and cumulative effort within organized castes or guilds, with continuity of work and tradition. And to them the definition and redefinition of suitable conduct, the formulation, maintenance and modifying of traditional belief, were more particularly committed than to their more ordinary fellows, who would normally take their cues from the chosen leaders. Opportunity for both study and speculative reflection was thus the prerogative, in especial measure, of individuals and groups religiously set apart, whether as chieftains, kings, lawgivers, or as priests, monks, or minor clergy.

And not only opportunity, but motive as well. For of all the practical adaptations early men are called upon to make, they conceive that none are of greater moment than commerce with gods and daemons, friendly and unfriendly. To the successful conduct of such intercourse, knowledge is requisite. This means partly, of course, knowledge of traditional ceremonies, incantations, injunctions and prohibitions—in short, of ritual acts and how to perform them; and learning in these matters may be imitative and repetitive rather than exploratory. Even when study has come to be the study of codes, precepts, and traditions elaborated into sacred literature, a discipline that may begin to claim the title of scholarship, the likelihood is great that its preoccupation with the past, with the traditionally correct, with the ceremonially fitting, will prevent its developing readily the objectivity and daring of free intellectual effort.

But another sort of knowledge also is sought in the name of religion: knowledge of the heavens and the earth, and of herbs, and of the fortunes of human living. Study of these matters, however befogged in guesswork and anthropomorphic prejudice its beginnings, and however closely bound at first to the mythologist's task of explaining hoary and half-unintelligible rites, has in it an urgent and limitless principle of advance. For its gaze includes things present and to come. In a relatively unmechanized society, living close to the earth, religion is not something apart from the everyday life of the community. It permeates all the activities of work and of war, of being born and coming of age, of living and dying. The spirit of religion, moreover, imbues these everyday affairs with urgency and mystery that can be a powerful stimulus to the effort to understand. The insistent present, the actual flow of health and disease, of time and seasons, of good fortune and bad, whether by gentle reiteration or by harsh insistence, urges on those that have eyes and ears the constant necessity of supplanting inadequate knowledge with more and better. In so far as religion, then, prompts men to study of nature and of human nature, it helps put them on the most promising road to intellectual maturity.

This is, of course, a very different thing from bringing them forthwith to the end of the road. The first thoughts of religious men about the stars and planets were mythologies that filled the heavens with persons and animals and implements of human life; and their second thoughts were systems of astrology that linked the movements of the celestial beings directly with events on the earth and in the lives of men. Mythology and astrology were, in different ways, man-centered, though they helped powerfully to stretch the imaginations and lift up the thoughts of men beyond the daily routine. The genuinely religious impulse in men, moreover, required in principle that men should move much farther along the difficult road of self-abnegation and learn to view reality in terms of its own being rather than in terms of their personal concerns. Astronomy could develop only among inquirers whose immediate concern was not to find manlike life among the stars, nor to find and to use star-influence among men, but to discover how the stars as stars behave. The first thoughts of religious men about health and disease, likewise, were mythological and magical. Evil daemons, malign influences and vapors bring sickness, and the cure is exorcism. Medicine men could become medical men only by outgrowing much that religious tradition had taught them. Earlier thoughts about human fortune were too much obsessed with taboos and inscrutable destinies, too little awake to the importance of individual character and conduct, and of dependable regularities in nature. The road from religious awe and aspiration to disinterested intellectual inquiry is a long one, the full length of which few men have traveled. But as far as we can judge, without religion the road would have been still longer. By helping to free some chosen men from routine labor, by lifting their thoughts from immediate economic needs to the stars and planets and the seasons and the duty and destiny of man, and by insuring to their work an exceptional measure of protection and continuity, organized religion has helped greatly to set the long quest on its way.

The ambivalent relationship between organized religion and free intellectual effort in the West is discernible throughout the period of clearly recorded history. The first full emergence of what we know as the sciences and philosophy in the West occurred among the Greek-speaking peoples of the eastern Mediterranean world. Among them, as many observers have noted, the association of religion and intellectual inquiry seems often to have been inseparably close, so close that coalescence or even identification rather than association seems the appropriate term. Pythagoreans study astronomy as a religious purification (*katharsis*) of the soul. Scientific medical study begins in the temples of Asclepius. Socrates pursues his ruthless career of enlightenment as a mission from the God of Delphi. Plato declares that profound study of astronomy and the other exact sciences must issue in piety, and no one can be truly devout who has not considered the rational order of the heavens. Some of the most influential and radical pre-Socratic philosophers —Heraclitus, Parmenides, not to mention Empedocles and lesser men—write in a strongly religious vein.

It is likely that all of the philosophical schools were organized as religious associations (*thiasoi*), a form that gave them recognized and protected legal status. For some of them, at least, the form was by no means an empty or perfunctory one, though some among them doubtless employed it merely for the sake of legal security. The followers of Aristotle or Epicurus, for example, were regarded by their contemporaries as less devout and more secular minded than the Pythagoreans, the Platonists, or the Stoics. Even among the Platonists, moreover, the temper of deep-going conviction fluctuated from generation to generation, with the Middle Academy preoccupied with fine-spun logic and the elaboration of highly sophisticated skepticism. But in Neoplatonism, the final heir to the tradition of the Academy in pagan circles, the religious impulse burns high once more; so that some of the bitterest opposition that early Christians had to meet came from intellectual aristocrats like Porphyry, whose adherents saw in Christianity a rival religion and fought it as an irrational and therefore a false alternative to their own. When the Emperor Julian, who had himself studied at the Academy in Athens, sought to replace Christianity with Neoplatonism, he was intending not to discredit religion but to replace a false religion with a true one.

In speaking thus of the philosophical schools in Greek territory, it is not to be forgotten that we are speaking of schools in which the mathematical and physical sciences first began to take clearly articulated form. It is well known that arithmetic, geometry, astronomy, and the study of harmonics were basic subjects in the curriculum of the Platonic Academy, and that of the accumulated mathematical wisdom summarized in Euclid's *Elements*, some of the most profound and vital theoretical portions were contributed by companions of Plato. Aristotle and his followers added the systematic study of zoology and botany. In the development of medical studies, whether following the tradition of the Pythagoreans or that of Hippocrates, a strong empirical or factual tendency was combined with a tendency almost equally strong to speculative theory. For us the important point is that the students of all these developing sciences take for granted the basic premises and the characteristic organizations of religious life. In becoming scientific inquirers, they do not cease to be religious men. Rather, they seek to construe the proper meaning of religion after the manner ascribed to Thales, in the judgment that divine power works in all events, not merely in some, in patterns of regularity rather than by caprice.

This last comment points up a situation among the Greeks that is so remarkable that two or three of its special conditions are worth noting. In the first place, in the Greek cities, observance of the traditional religion was a matter of civic responsibility. To worship the gods of Athens, and so to help insure the well-being of the city against both natural and human enemies, was a patriotic duty. It was for that reason that impiety (*asebeia*) was a capital offense, for in effect it was treason. Religion of this sort, then, was a function of the life of the community as a whole, and not a way of voluntary group life or a matter of individual conscience.

On the other hand, the religion practiced by such voluntary associations as the scientific and philosophical schools was tolerated, so long as the acts of individual members of these schools did not involve neglect or violation of civic duties. These minority groups, in some respects not unlike the sects familiar in Christian history, lived often enough under suspicion, ridicule, and sometimes persecution at the hands of their neighbors. Thus, the Pythagorean brotherhood in Croton was broken up, its leaders driven out, and one of its meeting-places burned with all but two of those who were in the house. Anaxagoras was forced out of Athens, and others who shared some of his views were lampooned by Aristophanes and hounded with abuse by other poets not now identifiable. Socrates, formally accused and condemned on a charge of impiety (that is, of treason) was put to death. Plato repeatedly portrays the philosopher as despised by worldlings. After Aristotle's death, his Peripatetic school was temporarily put to flight by a new Athenian law against "Sophists."

Most of this repressive activity is clearly chargeable to social conservatism, anti-rationalism, political rivalry, and other secular motives rather than to religion, even when religious grounds were alleged. Socrates seems clearly to have been condemned mainly on the ground of guilt by association—for example, with such genuine traitors as Alcibiades, and with the hated tyrants Critias and Charmides. He was the victim not of religious persecution but, as he himself clearly recognized in his speech of self-defense, of a deep-seated misunderstanding and cumulative hostility in the minds of the Athenian middle class, aggravated by the emotional effects of national disaster. In a calmer time and in a situation in which no such political motives were effective, as in the case of Aristotle's school, the charge of impiety was successfully retorted upon the attacker, and the restrictive law was repealed. In as far as these efforts at repression did involve traditional piety, religious motives and customs were operating on both sides of every conflict. The conflicts were not simply between religious authority and intellectual dissent. Rather, the conflicts were between one sort of religion and another. It seems not too much to say, indeed, that in more than one case the more obviously genuine religious conviction and devotion was on the side of the philosophic brotherhoods.

Their religious devotion, moreover, was not something separable from their philosophy. Rather, their intellectual efforts made articulate their religious conviction. It may be, indeed, that in the early Pythagorean school there were two factions, one committed to the keeping of primitive taboos, the other to mathematical and philosophical inquiry. But if that be true, intellectual inquiry was treated by the latter group as the best sort of "purification," so that the search for truth was itself the way of life. In these circumstances, philosophy need not lose its distinctive demand for clarity in gaining the passionate eagerness characteristic of full-blooded religion. Parmenides, Socrates, and Plato make that plain. For them philosophy is more than logic, but it can never disavow logic, and piety never requires that it shall. For such men, to seek the truth passionately is to be religious; and blessed are they who thus hunger and thirst, for they shall see the Good and be of all men most like God.

Where this strain in the Greek spirit made effective contact with Judaism, Christianity, and Islam, there appeared among them also vigorous intellectual advances in scholarship, in philosophy, and in the special sciences. The Jewish, Christian, and Muslim heirs of the Hellenistic tradition displayed powerful and authentic intellectual vitality, that long outlasted the cultural matrix of Hellenism itself. Moreover, each of them contributed distinctive and profound intellectual insights that deepened and broadened the currents of Greek wisdom. Non-Hellenic doctrines of creation, of time, of will, of personal existence, and of history have become a part of our Western heritage by reason of the insights furnished by these other religious traditions. At the same time, among them the naturalization of theoretic inquiry has almost never been as complete as in the religion of the Greek schools. For each of the three has been bound, from an early period in its career, to an authoritative scripture, with which all theory must conform; and the characteristic trailbreakers in these other religions were not dialecticians but prophets, whose new insights were announced mainly on other than intellectual grounds. However large a place each came to give to intellectual inquiry, therefore, it has been subjected in each to authoritative limits other than those of logic and ascertainable fact. Orthodox piety here, since in each instance it begins from an initial particular revelation, could never be simply identified with the philosophic or scientific quest.

For all that, devout Jews, Christians, and Arabs have amassed a record of intellectual achievement as impressive as it is familiar. There is little need to name over here the array of devoted thinkers in these three religious traditions without whom we should have no intellectual heritage worth the name. For the legacy of the ancient world was treasured and expanded in the schools of cathedral and monastery, synagogue and mosque in the new society that became modern Europe and America. Without the massive support of organized religion, it is hard to see how there could have been a recovery from the chaos that followed the downfall of the Roman Empire in the West.

Each of these great religious communities made distinctive contributions to the liberation and growth of the western mind; and each learned from both the others as well as from their common classical heritage. The blending of Greek and Jewish wisdom was foreshadowed in the *Wisdom of Solomon* a century before the Christian era, and was developed into an immense and subtle philosophy by Philo of Alexandria. Philo has a basic place in the rich flowering of Alexandrine thought in which late Platonism, Neo-Pythagoreanism, and Stoicism were variously fused with Jewish, Egyptian, Levantine, and Christian motifs, or by following another line developed into Neoplatonism, the maturest form of Greek thought and the classical base of most mediaeval and modern philosophies. Philo's closest successors were Christian thinkers and scholars—fellow-Alexandrines like Clement and Origen, who in turn helped to start a far-reaching intellectual movement in Syria and Asia Minor. Westward-moving Arabs learned from Syrian Christians, and in their turn gave a fresh impetus to Jewish thought, which reached new heights of systematic clarity and power in Saadia, Maimonides, and Spinoza. For each of these men, even the excommunicate Spinoza, Jewish monotheism was the indispensable groundwork of a powerful philosophic system.

The monotheism of Islam, likewise, reinterpreted in the terms of Aristotelian and Neoplatonic sources, developed imposing philosophic stature at the hands of Alkindi, Alfarabi, Avicenna, and Averroes, between 800 and 1200 the most encyclopedic thinkers west of the Indus. During a time when the Christan West was slowly recovering from the shock of the Roman collapse in the fifth century and civilizing an unwieldy mass of barbaric new peoples, the Arab masters and their Jewish contemporaries led the way in philosophy, and in the mathematical, physical, and medical sciences. For most of that time, on Christian soil in the West, the solitary, wayward genius of Eriugena alone could bear comparison with the teachers of Jewish and Muslim thought.

But once political and social stability had been reestablished in western Europe, with the organized Church as a chief rallying-point, there came a swift development of cathedral and monastic schools and the chartering of universities with multiple faculties for advanced study and teaching—Bologna in 1158, Paris in 1205, Oxford, Cambridge, Salamanca, and scores of others in a swiftly rising flood. The Christian intellectual enterprise had been solidly undergirded for Latin-speaking students before the fall of Rome by the philosophic, psychological, and theological genius of Augustine and the crabbed learning of Jerome. From the eleventh century, their work was taken up and carried forward with enthusiasm by an unbroken line of scholars and thinkers who began again with the problems of philosophic method, in Aristotle's *Organon,* and pushed on to new ventures of speculative daring— in the name of the God of truth. Some of them, like Eriugena, have always been viewed by churchly authorities with reserve or suspicion or perhaps condemned as heretics: Abailard, the Latin Averroists, Marsiglio, Ockham, Wyclif. Some have secure places of honor as men of weight and high intellectual power, though not among the saints—Grosseteste, Roger Bacon, Nicholas of Cusa, Jean Gerson. Some have been beatified or canonized who in their own day were daring innovators and radicals in thought: Anselm, Albert the Great, Thomas Aquinas, John Duns Scotus. All of them carried on their search for truth with zeal at once theoretic and religious.

With the rise of classical Humanism, the devotee as scholar turned in a new direction: to the intense study and interpretation of the texts of antiquity, pagan and Christian alike. Some of these devotees were neo-pagans, even though nominally Christian—chief among them the brilliant and arrogant Lorenzo Valla. But many Humanists, including many of the ablest—

Ficino, Agricola, Lefebevre, Erasmus—were devoutly religious men. The new Dutch schools of the Brethren of the Common Life were schools at once of modern learning and of piety. The Protestant Reformation began in the universities and established new universities—in Germany, Switzerland, the Low Countries, and the New World.

This record, which continues with important variations through the "modern" period of growing nationalism, social and ecclesiastical pluralism, relatively free enterprise, popular education, and immensely heightened prestige of the sciences and technology, does not mean that organized religion has uniformly favored freedom of the mind. It does mean that during a long period of precarious cultural development, organized religion has given indispensable support to organized intellectual inquiry, and that pioneering scientists, scholars, and philosophers have often been sustained in their inquiries by personal religious devotion.

The other side of the story is equally clear. When all due weight has been given to the familiar facts just noticed, it is necessary to recognize that organized religion at many times and places in the West, and in various ways has definitely hindered the development of free and mature intellectual life. The parent has been jealous of the child's attaining full stature; the quondam patron has mistrusted a ward grown to responsible freedom. Philosophy as a helper has been welcomed, but philosophy, science, and scholarship as outspoken critics and potential or actual rivals have often seemed intolerable.

The hampering influence of organized religion has been partly social and political, partly psychological. There has been a strong tendency to restrict advanced study and teaching to limited, authorized groups. In part this has merely given expression to the principle that only competent persons should be permitted to undertake difficult and socially important work; as a school of engineering or a faculty of law will decline, as a matter of course, to admit unqualified teachers or students. But over and above intellectual competence and acceptable character, organized religion has commonly sought to insist on a qualification of quite another sort. Whether it be called orthodoxy, conformity, correctness of belief, or something else, and however one may judge the values involved, the familiar fact is that when dogmatic agreement is imposed from without rather than developed from within, the effect on theoretical work is likely to be damaging. Similar restriction is, of course, by no means unknown outside the churches. Other organized groups have made and are making political or economic orthodoxy, for instance, prerequisite to acceptance in scientific or scholarly posts; and the effect on disinterested intellectual work has been similarly bad. Under such conditions, it is the most original and creative minds that are likely to suffer most, unless they are sufficiently self-confident and powerful to break through the restrictions.

Such restrictions are sometimes imposed, by organized religion as well as by political and industrial associations, in fairly crude ways. The most obvious way to try to curb independent inquiry directly is to resort to censorship or to persecution. That is, of course, the reverse side of the effort to ensure that study and teaching shall be carried on by thinkers of approved orthodoxy. Censorship seeks to prevent materials for study from falling into the hands of unauthorized persons, and to prevent unauthorized teaching. When censorship fails, as in some measure it usually does, there may be resort to persecution or some other sort of coercion, which seeks not merely to forestall certain acts but to intimidate, to remove, or otherwise to disable persons who may be guilty or suspected of such acts—in this instance, of unauthorized study or teaching.

Much more subtle and far-reaching, though less overtly repressive, are various psychological restrictions which organized religion has frequently imposed. In many ways, often without intending to do so, it reinforces powerfully the everyday human motives—preference for the familiar, caution, lethargy, enjoyment of vested interests, and the like—which tend to keep inquiry within fixed bounds. First, religion has almost universally conferred the sanction of sacredness upon what has been from of old. On the credit side, we have seen how this tendency has operated to the advantage of traditionalistic learning, giving it protected standing-room in the press of economic urgencies. But one can see how it must operate also to the curbing of free inquiry, by reserving from critical examination and possible displacement certain customs, ceremonies, sacred books, dogmas, official persons or castes; and by discountenancing inquiry believed to bring any of these into discredit, or to detract from their prestige and authority. Objection on this score is likely to be directed not just to intellectual activity as such, but to disturbing innovation of any sort. Prophets who criticize the established order in the name of true piety itself, on the strength of non-intellectual revelations, have been assailed no less promptly than rationalistic scholars— sometimes more promptly. But taken by and large, intellectual inquiry has been severely hindered by this sanctification of the traditional, even when it has not issued in overt repression. Conservatism and continuity with the past are indispensable for dependable personal and intellectual growth. But too uniform a preference for the *status quo* makes a mental atmosphere ill-suited to vigorous work.

Further, if judged by the standard of the freest, maturest, most disinterested inquiries man has performed, much religious thinking has been vitiated by too constant subordination to ulterior practical demands. Religion itself is, in an important sense, predominantly practical in its aims, and like other practical pursuits—political, industrial, medical, pedagogical, social—it tends naturally, and not without justification, to seek practical gains from inquiry carried out under its auspices. But just as continual preoccupation with practical results in these other fields can turn the fine edge of research, whether in history, chemistry, physiology, or what not, so religious preoccupation which forever urges the thinker to find what shall be edifying, consoling, or somehow spiritually useful, rather than just to find what is the case, is more than likely to shorten his perspectives, narrow his purview, and deflect his line of vision.

Such is the equivocal record of the influence of organized religion on systematic intellectual inquiry in the West. The beginnings and much of the growth of the intellectual disciplines have indubitably been fostered by organized religion without whose protection and utility-transcending motivation such inquiry would hardly have found room as it did in the human struggle for survival. At their most advanced stages, too, intellectual life and organized religion have often been most intimately associated. But flagrant contrariety marks the whole course of their association. For on the one hand, some of the best Western thought has been achieved in the name and under the stimulus of religious aspiration. On the other, some of the best Western thinkers have been hampered, vilified, and condemned in the name of religious orthodoxy.

In part this confusion is to be explained by recognizing that in so far as religion is embodied in institutions, it has shared the ambivalent tendencies of human institutions generally. Social pressure such as organized religion has employed against daring thinkers is employed also, we have noted, for essentially similar reasons by political and economic organizations. These reasons are not merely obstructionist. Human associations are usually formed in the first instance to promote the realization of ends they regard as having positive value, and their purpose includes both the stimulation of endeavor, and the conservation of gains achieved. If gains are not to be lost, a substantial measure of consolidation and resistance to change is obviously needed; just as in the individual life, the fruits of learning must be consolidated into habits or else continuously slip away. At the same time, this indispensable social consolidation and conservation, like habit, becomes increasingly rigid with age, until the adventurousness and adaptability that characterize a youthful, pioneering organization are largely displaced by stereotyped behavior. Not only age but size, too, plays an important part. Small organizations or the constituent units of decentralized ones can react more quickly and venture more readily than large ones with ponderous machinery and complex responsibilities, for which a misstep is much harder to make right. With age and size, moreover, come vested interests, caution, and the dangers associated with power. So that all things considered, the transition from legitimate conservation of value achieved to obstinate refusal to move toward new values is perilously easy to make—all the more if the *status quo* has been won at great cost and hallowed by great names. For when later generations seek to defend objectives already won, they easily forget that their heroes were most heroic as liberators, not as despots, and that their aims, if high enough, remain forever not yet achieved. In these familiar conditions of organized living, religious institutions have shared, for better and for worse.

But deeper than these difficulties incident to social organization, there is an essential polarity in concrete religious life itself, that appears and persists in all varieties and at all levels. Religion seeks insight, but also it begins and apparently must live face to face with mystery. It continually reaches beyond what here and now is given, yet it craves security and repose. It is a source both of liberating, mold-shattering effort, and of insistence upon submission, humility, discipline. The free spirit and the word of authority, God who is Light and God as Mystery go in some way together in all the great religions. It is little wonder that their relationship to theoretical inquiry has been so full of paradox.

So long, moreover, as men are actual experimenting beings and not abstract formulae, I presume that conflicts of "science" and "religion" will continue, on shifting fronts; and so will conflicts of science with science and of religion with religion. For such conflicts are not between abstract verities, to be either treated as ultimate or resolved by definition. They are between more or less clear-headed men, engaged in exploring and judging a still mysterious universe. Growth seems to come that way, and one need not wholly regret it.

But in our day, as in the days of the early church against the pagan empire and in the time of the revolt against feudalism in the West, another word needs to be spoken. In most parts of the West, the power and (one may hope) the will to apply crude force has already passed in large measure from the hands of organized religion to those of organized politics, business, and patriotism. These are now the chief heresy hunters, and religion itself, in its most vital and authentic forms, stands again in danger of persecution at their hands. That position it shares with free intellectual inquiry, which I suppose is always and everywhere under suspicion among rulers who fear change. In that common plight, which seems likely to be of long duration, it seems not fantastic to hope that organized religion may come increasingly to make common cause with the freest and maturest intellectual inquiry against short-sighted, earth-bound tyrannies of every kind.

Religion's Role in Liberal Education

NATHAN M. PUSEY

THE PRESENT CONDITION of our national life seems to many to present a serious threat to freedom of thought. Our current situation has a curious double character. Viewed in its surface aspect it is disturbed, confused, and uncertain. When we look at some people, we are struck by their apparent fear, resentment, anger, and vindictiveness. When we look at others, we meet apathy, unconcern, and a readiness to put up with almost any evil if only they can be let alone. But there are also bits of evidence to suggest that beneath this ambiguous surface strong constructive forces are at work. Indeed they may be marshaling for a new advance. Promising attacks are now being made in many quarters on juvenile delinquency. There are resolute if inconspicuous efforts toward fundamental and improved constructions in international relations. A great variety of basic research is being carried on in many universities. Above all, perhaps, the widened, lively new interest in religion founded less in fear than in hope and deeper understanding bespeaks the presence of faith and gives the lie to those who would see only defeat and frustration in the present time.

But the surface aspect *is* disturbing. We in the universities cannot help but be very conscious of it, because of the many recent public criticisms and attacks directed at those working in education. To set this unpleasant characteristic of our time before us a little more clearly, it may be helpful to draw a parallel with a somewhat similar period of social tension, recrimination, and strife strikingly described by Thucydides more than two thousand years ago. Thucydides had an exceptional gift for seeing the general in the particular. The *kind* of thing we have been witnessing, which may be a social illness we have even today learned only very imperfectly to understand, seems intimately to have been known by him. It may also be the part of wisdom if we share his assumption that such unpleasant periods will probably continue to recur.

In such times of social turmoil—to paraphrase the words of Thucydides —passion takes the place of reason; cunning supplants openness; and accusation, lying, and self-seeking proliferate. The boisterous, uncouth, and uninhibited fellow comes into increased prominence and wins respect. Violence is mistaken for manliness; thoughtful consideration and the judicious weighing of public issues are taken as signs of cowardice. Tempers rise. Things are all black and white and simple, and there is little or no effort to see sides of a question other than one's own. Individuals animated by a lust for power —we might also add, by vindictiveness and by greed and ambition—pass themselves off as public champions and make—and here I quote directly— "fair use of phrases to arrive at guilty ends." There follows an ascending extravagance of claim and counter-claim. Reason, fair-mindedness, regard for truth, justice—these things depart. Along with them go decency, honor, freedom of thought. One might almost say that thought itself goes too, except for that cunning kind of thought which is used to obscure truth and even to establish untruth.

There are clearly points of similarity between the situation Thucydides was describing and our own. Both were periods of serious social illness. In such times reasonable behaviour is conspicuous by its absence. Some people behave blatantly, defiantly in disregard of charity, justice, and decency; others, failing in courage or concern, show too little disposition to discriminate, to pass judgment, and to stand against violence. Just as in Thucydides' time the path to freedom of thought was uncertain, so it is again today. And there is a consequent need, therefore, now, as then, to take thought for it; for (as Thucydides knew and described elsewhere, in the words of Pericles' funeral oration) freedom of thought has a curious and unrivaled power to release creative energy both within individuals and in states and so to work for increase and health.

It is perhaps because we have been inclined recently to take freedom of thought for granted that it now comes as a shock to find this great good seriously threatened by intractability and anger on the one hand, and by indifference on the other. The upsurging forces of restraint, as they affect education, seem to have arisen in resentment and reaction against a real or imagined earlier excess of unrestraint in educational procedures. But whatever the cause, there are again among us a very large number of people, many surely with more fervor than perceptiveness, eager to impose upon education various new restrictive orthodoxies and to curtail free discussion and adventure.

This repressive spirit shows itself at many points: in a spate of books and articles attacking practices in the public schools; in renewed efforts to require special oaths of teachers; in attempts on the part of persons other than those professionally concerned to legislate or to dictate what may or may not be taught; in efforts, in community after community, to curb and restrain, and to make teaching "safe."

That this reaction springs from resentment rather than from reason or concern for justice should be apparent, however, to even the tardy observer. Let me cite only one example. An especially determined and careful effort made to uncover subversives in one university by people who "knew" they were there, could find to be questioned just four individuals—only one of whom had a continuing relationship to the institution. And yet this university has at present a teaching and research staff of three thousand and can count many more thousands who had taught there during the approximately two decades under review. The story elsewhere has been very much the same. Thus, despite much innuendo and reiterated accusation, what the investigations of the colleges and universities have demonstrated about American education is not that it stands in need of censorship and restraint, but rather that the loyalty and devotion of the teaching profession are substantial and pervasive.

Yet the hostile public clamor has gone on for more than a year, and still continues. What effect has it had on freedom of thought within the colleges and universities? It was Whitehead, I believe, who pointed out that one of the greatest advantages of undergraduate life is its irresponsibility. By this he meant the traditional freedom of undergraduates to assume and experiment with all sorts of intellectual attitudes and systems of thought without that concurrent restricting responsibility with which full-fledged adults are burdened to make their ideas work in the world. Of course this kind of irresponsibility can be and sometimes is overdone. But at least in some measure, when it is genuine, such irresponsibility is also an almost essential aid to learning and to the development of free minds. It should not lightly be forsworn—now or ever—in an effort to placate critics of higher education who, understanding little of how education works or what it is trying to do, or of the origin of the priceless advantages a free intellectual life contributes, are inclined to feel that young people should not be so much encouraged to think, or drawn into thinking, as given sets of "answers."

It is idle to deny that there has been some lessening of this kind of irresponsibility on college campuses as a consequence of recent criticism. Caution, hesitation, even, in a few unfortunate cases, a mean-minded calculation as to how best in a material sense "to get on in the world"—these things seem to be at least a little more in evidence now than they used to be. They are poison both to the happy idealism which young people are normally so ready to display and to the excited, free play of young minds with the world's store of ideas. In some measure, as has been suggested, this is perhaps a natural and inevitable reaction to recent earlier excess. But such a consideration should never lead to the assumption that restriction, the fear of making mistakes, the refusal to take chances, the desire at all costs to escape notice—qualities quite unbecoming in young people—are good things in themselves, that they are to be cultivated, or that they have much to contribute to the production of free men. It is unfortunate if most of us carry inside of us by nature, like chameleons, a protective coloring of timidity behind which we take refuge in the face of violently hostile criticism, however unenlightened it may be. At the moment this coloring may have some claim to fashion on college campuses. Yet the work of the university goes on.

What is this work, and how does it relate both to the present trouble and to religion? The university's task is to conduct research and to advance knowledge, yes; but even more, it is to train the men to do such work, to lead them to want to do it, to give them free and ready minds. Beneath, around, in, and through every part of a college's or university's activity is the responsibility for liberal education. In other words it is the central mission of the college and university working together—indeed in a sense of the whole process of formal education—to produce men and women capable of practicing freedom of thought. One cannot remain in a true university or college and pretend that this is not so. And this points to a central consideration.

Quite without that kind of assistance from outside the university world, which is now so distressingly before us, freedom of thought is always in peril. Indeed our minds are caught by nature and the conditions of our early years in a vast network of limitation. The most prominent strand in this network may be lack of knowledge, but there are others scarcely less formidable: lack of energy, dilatoriness, inadequate imaginative capacity, mistaken or narrow purpose, too little endurance or courage, too little aspiration, too little concern, too little commitment of the whole self—these and other widespread, perennial restrictions from which it is the true and constant business of liberal education to endeavor to set minds free. Such interior restraining strands are very numerous and very powerful, and we must seek in them rather than in external force the explanation for both the extravagance and the insufficiency of current actions in the present painful social disturbance. For it is their crippling effect, not external compulsion, that chiefly causes our efforts repeatedly to fall short of constructive achievement, not least in time of crisis.

At the moment, as individuals we are uneasy; society is disturbed. Some of us have been and remain lost in apathy, indifference, even cynicism, completely lacking in resolution. Others sin through zealotry. There is very little quiet confidence and trust, too little awareness of limitation on the one hand, too little energy and caring on the other. Has education itself no responsibility for this?

It is possible to contend, as many have done, that these failures owe at least something to an excessive preoccupation in recent educational practice with a single avenue to truth that too often leads away from relevance. Perhaps as a consequence of our devotion to a single method some of the things upon which the human spirit should feed have been withheld or, at best, supplied in inadequate amounts. Imagination, questing, awareness, these are important. It is possible they have been too little consciously sought after, too little cultivated. And beyond them, a sense of wholeness, a conviction of relatedness leading to lively concern for others, and to the desire and courage to stand—are not these too capacities we may rightfully expect liberal education to contribute, indispensable related goods that should come with knowledge? In any event, our major present failures both as men and in social organization seem to spring less from the knowing parts of our minds or from a lack in our knowledge about things than from inadequate imagination and from inability to act in the light of our knowledge.

There is a very pressing need in the world of thought, and in all of our lives, for more of those flashes of insight that let minds break through beyond external, isolated, and unengaging fact to deeper, more exciting meanings foreshadowed there. Such aesthetic experiences speak to our hearts and wills and kindle thought. And beyond them there is the very great need for an enduring meaning which will pick us up, give us a sense that we belong and carry responsibility, lift us above partiality, give us confidence, and make us care.

Art, poetry, music, and letters—these things speaking the language of myth and symbol—have a peculiar educational value, an ability to strike into inner self where mind, heart, and will can be brought together. This has been consciously known at least from Plato's time. It has probably been experienced almost from the beginning of the human story. It has been demonstrated again and again, as all who have felt the claim of art can testify. It will be a pity if we do not have more such experiences now, for there is a source of power in them at least to begin one's emancipation from purposelessness and unconcern, as from violence. But this process will not do its work, nor will it endure, if it stops here.

What every young person seeks in college, from liberal education— whether or not he has articulated this—is self-discovery. What he wants most to know is what it means to be a human being, what is expected of him as such, what the world is, and what are the options in it that lie before him, and how he is to get on with others. In short, the really burning question that faces someone trying to live through his mind is *what is he to do with his life?* What such a person wants—what we all want—is a meaning that becomes a motivating force in our lives. And when we ask this question, whether we are conscious of it or not, we have begun to think religiously, and have begun to ask of God. I see no reason not to admit that this is so.

Yet there has long been a widespread feeling in university circles that religion does not belong. It has been accepted almost as axiomatic that religion, or at any rate organized religion, instead of being an aid to free intellectual activity and to fullness of life, is a major foe. It is said that it is hostile to the untrammeled pursuit of truth and freedom, because it has a special, limited truth, a narrow range of interest of its own which it wishes to impose.

The origin of this mistrust of religion within the universities is probably to be found in the fact that they often had to develop into great instruments for advancing knowledge, not only without much encouragement from those who professed to speak for religion, but indeed in the very face of their active and open opposition. It is undeniable that seriously restrictive forces injurious to free thought did then and still lie within organized religion. And this condition will probably continue; for men do not cease to be men when they join churches.

Let us make a necessary concession: The record of religion in the development of great universities in the United States during the past eighty years was not always one to engender confidence in its disinterested concern for the pursuit of truth, or to suggest that there is always and inevitably within everything that passes under the name of religion a capacity to draw out men's minds and hearts into knowledge and charity. Too often the evidence pointed, and points, the other way. But this is no answer to our present need. When we look at the troubled state of the present world—the kind of world Thucydides described and we know all too well—one thing becomes manifest. This is the failure of recent educational practice to prepare men in terms of heart and will and mind to prevent the strife, misunderstanding, and willfulness that now arise, or constructively and resolutely to cope with them once arisen.

It would seem then that a time has come again to make the attempt that religion makes, to seek once more for an education that will address itself to the whole person—not any less to minds, but also to hearts and wills. Though we recognize that those professing religion can be as insensitive and resistant to grace as any others, this does not excuse us from the necessity to be concerned for it if we are to teach whole men to be receptive to the goods which aesthetic awareness and religious experience can alone bestow. I refer to the sense of relevance and richness and purpose in the world, to reverence, and to that belief necessary for the trust and creative concern for others which are as much the outward signs as they are the inner glory and the motivation of the fully liberated man. What we are concerned for here is the ability, and the desire, in the strain and stress of life, to walk humbly, constructively, prayerfully, and hopefully with God.

Without faith, without some glimpse of the meaning of Christ, there is much evidence to suggest one must always face life and all crises in terms merely of his own temperament. So some will give up. Others will insist. But education cannot turn away from its responsibility to try to help people to a *reasonable* sense of meaning in life—more especially to an awareness of meaning in their lives, of meaning, and of responsibility. Trust, awareness, concern, the power to stand—whence will these come—this is our question—if we focus attention on anything less than God's truth or fail to feel its sustaining strength?

I come back now to Thucydides' picture and to our experience of a disturbed society. If there is indeed, because of fear, a lessening of the practice of freedom today in schools, colleges, and elsewhere, it is a little too easy to blame this on the present public clamor. If there is now a resurgence of restraint, and of inhibiting, even destructive force working upon educational institutions, and at the same time too little sense of danger, too little will to resist or to find a constructive answer, this may be a kind of judgment on these institutions. Clearly if these forces exist—as in some instances they seem to do—they exist also in the minds of people who themselves have had the full advantage of experience at these educational institutions. And if then it is our ambitious boast that we work to make society reasonable, when we fail it would seem only fair that we bear at least some of the responsibility for the failure and honestly ask ourselves how we might do better.

We in the world of education cannot just demand intellectual freedom with any hope that society will accord it to us. Nor can we compel it. We have to win it. We have to win it again and again. We can win it only by practicing it fully and continuously, and by demonstrating its power for good so that all those outside the colleges will be happy to let freedom live and do its work within. Some protections against arbitrary and willful interference are accorded us by law and custom. Perhaps there should be more of these; at least we might hope that any present tendency to whittle away at such protections can be stopped. But beyond this, freedom—or rather the absence of irritating, misguided restriction—can be expected to be accorded to education only as education wins understanding and respect. It will not come through appeasement nor through unworthy compromise; neither through any effort to buy off criticism, nor through pretentious assertion of right. It will come only through a convincing demonstration of why this kind of freedom should be accorded educational institutions for their personal, and so for the public, good.

In the midst of the present turmoil and confusion, it is easy to discern an immense task immediately before us. We are perhaps unnecessarily innocent if we do not recognize that this task will always remain, that ours is a continuing responsibility to be discharged quietly, resolutely, and confidently, without wasting energy in crying out vindictively against opposition. There is nothing very new, nor very terrifying, in the situation in which we find ourselves, as Thucydides' passage may have served to show. But we—all of us—will stand in need of faith to get on with the job, and indifference to religion in the world of education would therefore seem—whatever the situation may have been a generation or more ago—at least now to be a luxury we can no longer afford.

There is a further consideration. We are responsible, at least in some measure, through inadequate performance for some of our present difficulties. In a sense it may be that we were suffering from innocence or complacency, and that the present public clamor which seems at first glance to be so restrictive and menacing may in fact be the beginning of our deliverance, and provide both the occasion and the incentive to the recovering of freedom. Intellectual freedom is not an idol to be venerated. It is rather a manner of acting, a great good created only as it is lived and practiced. The attack under which educational institutions seem now to be gives them again a real situation in which to inquire what freedom is, to see what responsibility it bears with it, what its ingredients are. Here is an opportunity not just to laud freedom but to live it. It is perhaps therefore an advantage—not a source for regret—that we are now called upon again not so much to genuflect when we hear the name of freedom, as to try to be free men. It may indeed be that a time not only for polite interest and discussion, but even more for rebirth and resurgence is at hand.

Freedom, education, and religion. I have tried to suggest that freedom is the real goal of education but that it will not be won without an undergirding of religious experience. When the human mind and heart are brought together in a supporting relationship, when the whole person is lifted up and extricated not just from lack of knowledge, but also from lack of meaning, from limited purpose, from failure of concern, then, by whatever name we call it, religious experience is under way. Of this we have present need in the colleges. For only with this kind of awakening to God's purpose is there likely to be an enduring desire and the courage to stand for freedom, to work patiently against the recurrent restrictions both within and without universities that strive always in opposition to God to hold back the spirit of man.

The Commitment of the Self and the Freedom of the Mind

REINHOLD NIEBUHR

W HEN CONSIDERING the problem of freeing the mind, we are too prone to think first of the various political and social restraints upon the free play of man's rational faculty. It would be more helpful to consider first the inner restraints which the self places upon its mind; for the mind is not a simple sovereign of the self, but the servant. It is one of the illusions of a rationalistic age that the mind would control the self, if only irrelevant political restraints were not intervening. The fact is that the processes of the mind are very much colored either by the self's own interests or by its commitments and loyalties. These commitments may redeem the self from itself, but they do not necessarily emancipate its mind, for the self's commitments may be as restrictive upon the mind as its interests. In other words, if we define religion as the self's commitment to some system of meaning, or its loyalty to some scheme of values, we must accept the fact that there is a basic contradiction between religion and the freedom of the mind. This contradiction is not due to the baneful effects of what modern men term religious "dogma." It operates just as effectively within the lives of very modern "emancipated" people who have disavowed every kind of "explicit dogma," but are nevertheless governed by "implicit dogmas." In the case of communism, the dogma is of course very explicit, but pretends to be implicit in the sense that the communist faith pretends to be the conclusion arrived at by a "scientific" inquiry into the facts of history.

Modern culture exhibits all the characteristics of the Biblical parable of the "house swept and garnished," of the man, free of one devil into whose empty life there entered "seven devils more evil than the first," and "the last estate of that man was worse than the first." In other words, political commitments of religious dimensions have entered the emptiness of uncommitted lives. Man is the kind of creature who cannot be whole except he be committed, because he cannot find himself without finding a center beyond himself. In short the emancipation of the self requires commitment.

But it must be apparent to any student of religious history that these commitments quite frequently restrict the freedom of the mind unduly. They prevent it from analyzing the facts of life which would seem not to fit into the picture of life created by the primary religious loyalty. The story of religious fanaticism is the story of religious loyalties so restrictive as to present false visions of reality which make it impossible for the "religious" person to live in mutuality and respect with any person not sharing his religious commitments.

We cannot deny that there is a real problem of religious tolerance, even in communities long accustomed to the standard of toleration. The fact of religious fanaticism confronts us with two problems: 1) how can we prevent the religious commitment from being unduly restrictive, and 2) how can we establish community with those who have different religious loyalties than our own?

The obvious, but too simple, answer to the first question is that the religious loyalty which has God, rather than some idol, as the object of its worship is not restrictive. The only really restrictive religion is idolatry, the worship of some false god such as the nation or class or any contingent value which the false religion endows with ultimate significance.

There is indeed a great difference between obviously idolatrous religions, such as communism, and the rigorously monotheistic religions, such as Judaism and Christianity, who worship a creator and redeemer God whose majesty and holiness judges all partial and particular interests, and convicts men of their inclination to exalt themselves above measure. Logically this kind of faith should eliminate all fanaticism and make for humility and charity. Actually there is a long history of fanaticism and uncharitable strife between the various versions of our Biblical faith, Jewish and Christian, Catholic and Protestant. Why could these things happen? Religious fanaticism in the name of a rigorous monotheism is obviously possible only because men falsely identify historically contingent values with the God of their own devotion. It is this inclination which makes religion so dangerous; though one must hasten to add that the inclination cannot be overcome by abolishing "religion." In that case we merely get the greater corruption of the modern political "pseudo-religions." It is in other words simply the inclination of the human heart to ascribe absolute significance to contingent and partial values and interests, and to do so even within the framework of a religion which exalts one God above these lesser "gods." This inclination makes it necessary to sharpen the critical intelligence, so that the mind be not too restricted by the self's commitments, and the self be constantly challenged to prove that the values, which it exalts in the name of God, are in fact true values and legitimate loyalties. It is at this point where there must be a meeting between the high religion which commits the self and a responsible culture which attempts to "free the mind." Ideally, a liberal culture should know that it is not dealing with discarnate minds but with selves who are and must be committed. And faith must know the human heart well enough to understand that every kind of intellectual as well as religious discipline is necessary to prevent the self from identifying its cherished loyalties and commitments too simply with the supreme God of its devotion.

The second question, how we establish community with people who have different commitments from our own, is partly answered with the answer to the first question. A measure of humility, charity, and tolerance is the prerequisite of such community. Consistently fanatic faiths destroy community. There must be some suspicion that there may be error in my way of stating the truth and that there must be some truth in what seems to me to be the error of the other person before we can arrive at stable community.

It is interesting however that the fact of community between various religious sects does more to broaden the base of religious commitment than purely religious or intellectual disciplines do to provide a broad enough base for such community. This is the fact which makes the history of religiously heterogeneous communities so inspiring. The community taught the religions to moderate their pretensions. Modern democratic nations have achieved religious, among other liberties, not because there were many religious people who thoroughly believed in liberty. Only a few independents in 17th century England had a genuine devotion to liberty. And in America, Roger Williams, Thomas Jefferson, and James Madison had this devotion. Fortunately, religious sects proliferated beyond anyone's contriving. The thesis of European civilization since the treaty of Westphalia was that the community would be imperiled, if it was not supported by religious uniformity. But given the plurality of sects, it became apparent to even the most obtuse that the effort to establish religious uniformity by coercion would harm the community more than the hazardous venture of toleration. Most of our founding fathers genuinely believed in freedom, but they were able to establish religious liberty in our nation largely because those who did not could see the futility of any alternative policy. In this, as in the establishment of all our democratic liberties, the providential workings in history were much more effective than the conscious contriving of men. It was a case of God making "the wrath of man to praise Him."

It must be conceded that the religious commitments in a community cannot be too sharply contradictory. In India, the contrast between the Hindu and Moslem faith has made a unified national community impossible. In our own country the wide divergencies between the three forms of faith, rooted in a common scripture, were fortunately not so great as to furnish contrasting testimony on the nature of our common life. We have, therefore, been able to build a common life in spite of great diversity in our religious commitments and ethnic loyalties; and the community has been richer because of its multifarious components. It may be more important that the religious life has been the purer, because the pretensions of each group have been moderated by the inevitable challenge which they met in this uncoerced togetherness. In short the "mind" of each religious group was freed by the necessity of coming to terms with other groups whose virtues may have proved that virtue is not the monopoly of any of the other groups, as was presupposed in their too self-righteous presuppositions, and whose particular approaches to problems of community tended to correct deficiencies and weaknesses in the approach of other groups. Thus for instance the capacity for civic virtue in the Jewish minority group will be a perpetual reproof to the pretensions of Christian groups that their faith may be the only basis of civic righteousness; or the devotion to the moral law of non-Catholic Christian groups must be a reminder to Catholic Christians that their definition of the "natural law" is not the only valid source of the consciousness of law beyond our interests. It may even correct the tendency to define law too narrowly.

A free society manages in fact to draw upon the virtues, and to correct the vices, of various components of the community by counterwailing influences of other components. The mind of each religious group is freed by these democratic pressures in exactly the same way as interest groups of various kinds are purged of the virulence of their bias, by the challenge which they must meet from other groups. In this situation, the democratic consensus, without which a community cannot survive, must be tentative and precarious; and the required majority, necessary for common action, may be composed from time to time by the most various alliances of groups. But history has proved the consequences in justice to be much higher in this freedom than is possible to attain when the "truth" about justice, as defined by any one religious group or, for that matter, any interest group, remains unchallenged. This is true because the mind by which we define justice is bound, not only by ultimate commitments, but by immediate interests. There is no better way of freeing these various minds than the way which has been found in a free society. They would have, if left unchallenged, attempted to dominate the community and provide it with the only ultimate definition of "truth" and "justice."

The history of free societies proves conclusively that the dictum that "error" does not have the same rights as the "truth" is a very dangerous one, not because it is not possible to distinguish between truth and error, but because, in the endless conflicts of interest in a society, it is dangerous to give any interest group the monopoly to define the "truth." So much truth rides into history on the back of error, and so much "error" is but a neglected portion of the whole truth, which is an error only in the degree that it has been overemphasized in order to get itself heard and when acknowledged and restored to the whole, ceases to be an error and becomes a part of the truth. Catholicism, for instance, long since defined the idea of the socialization of property to be an error; and so it has proved to be. But would the error of justice embodied in a feudal society have been corrected, except by political forces which partly believed in this error? Ideally the Church, which defines what is truth or error, is not itself one of the forces, contending in society for an advantage, but is a transcendent community, above all contending forces. All of us who are Christians, believe that the church holds the "Oracles of God,"—that is, that it is a community of grace, testifying to the final truth about life as given in the Christian revelation. But would the fact that this transcendent community is also an interest group, through the sins and interests of its members, have ever been fully disclosed except in a freedom which also allowed the church to be challenged on its ultimate truth? In this case the truth could not be purged of the error which adhered to it, except by challenges which challenged the truth itself.

As an illustration of the wholesome effect of these challenges, it might be worth calling attention to the difference in the life of Catholicism in nations in which its truth remains unchallenged—as for instance, in Spain and in Latin America—and in western European nations, more particularly in France and in the German Rhineland, in which the church is not in a dominant position, but in which it is a more genuine community of grace than where it holds a monopoly of power. We reach the ironic conclusion from this comparison that the truth of the church is the purer in those nations where it is possible to challenge it as error. Moreover it becomes a more transcendent religious community in those nations in which it is frankly one of the contending political forces, than in situations in which human pretensions in the name of religion remain unchallenged.

We thus arrive at the conclusion that the most effective way of freeing the mind of restraints placed upon it by corruptions in its religious commitments is to have enough political freedom to challenge these corruptions. Political freedom is thus a necessary instrument for the attainment of the inner freedom which the mind needs above and beyond its religious commitments.

II

We have considered thus far how the "mind" may be emancipated from too restrictive religious commitments and have found that the devotion to the one God who is our creator and redeemer is not a guarantee of such emancipation, because so many historic and contingent interests insinuate themselves into this devotion. We have noted that only political freedom with the consequent right to challenge the combination of ultimate and immediate commitments in which historic religions abound is adequate to purge even the "truest" religion of its historic corruptions.

We have assumed the truth in the attitude of religious commitment, however, and have limited our analysis to a consideration of freeing the "mind" of too restrictive religious commitments. We must now include the efforts of a so-called "secular culture" to free the mind by the ordinary disciplines of science and education. These efforts might well be interdicted from the standpoint of the "truth" as apprehended by Christian faith. They are infected with error, not only because they fail to acknowledge the reality of God, but because they persist in obscuring the human self in all of its majesty or misery. They either equate the self with mind, and therefore trust "enlightenment" to accomplish its emancipation, or they deny that even the mind of the self is significant, and insist on reducing the self to an object in nature. Some grave consequences flow from these errors. The rise of totalitarian political religions prove, on the one hand, that the self is a self which must be committed, and that it will break through "enlightenment" and all the prudence of a scientific culture to give itself to the various devils and idols of history. They prove, on the other hand, that it is dangerous to rob the self of its dignity and regard it merely as an instrument of a political program or a communal purpose. Why should not these efforts of freeing the mind be interdicted since they lead so inevitably into a new kind of slavery? The simple answer to this question is that they should not be suppressed because there is so much truth contained in their errors and it is so necessary to free the mind by purely rational processes, however futile a purely rational approach to the problem of human selfhood may be. Our so-called free societies have been developed not only by the freedom of various religious groups to challenge each other, but by the freedom of secular and religious disciplines to challenge and to complement each other.

Our whole "liberal arts" education is built upon this uneasy tension between secular disciplines having their origin in the Renaissance, and religious disciplines having their origin in the Reformation. In fact, the processes of education with their inevitable emphasis on science and philosophy have rather favored the Renaissance against the Reformation, and have frequently relegated religion to an outmoded "pre-scientific" mode of thought and life. But meanwhile, they did, by a rational analysis of all the sequences and coherences of the world of nature and history, encourage the mind of man to comprehend the total mystery and meaning of human existence, and have emancipated the mind from the "superstitions" to which previous religious ages were undoubtedly prone. They have emphasized casual sequence and coherence, and thereby obscured the deeper mystery of creation. They have emphasized rational coherence, and thereby they have obscured the unique human self, involved on the one hand in the "incoherence" of his sin, and on the other hand in the incoherence of "grace," of forgiveness, and redemption. For these ultimate dimensions of human selfhood there is no place in any philosophy or any science, and certainly not in a naturalistic one.

Yet a secular culture which spread these errors about man also contributed to the truth. Without its disciplines, religion could not have been emancipated from its penchant for elaborating its picture of the world in ways which defied all the facts to which scientific accounts of reality gave witness, all of the "structures" which furnish the skeleton of nature and also of human nature. Even when they were most grievously in error, these disciplines contributed to the truth about man, the one entity in the world which they misunderstood most grievously.

Consider, for instance, the discipline of modern psychology, particularly modern depth psychology. Freud denied the reality of human freedom, and all his expositions suffer from the restrictive character of his naturalistic presuppositions. These narrow and erroneous presuppositions inevitably betray Freudianism into nonsense, not only on the ultimate religious levels of human nature (where the problem of guilt is dissolved into the problem of neurotic guilt feelings), but also on the political level on which the monstrous power impulses of historic communities are analyzed as merely the cumulations of the "aggressive" tendencies of individuals. No more naïve approach to political evil can be imagined. Yet this same Freudianism, purged by experience of some of its worst aberrations, has become the basis of a very creative psychotherapy which has cured many people of ills, the causes of which were hitherto so obscure that the ills were not really known as ills.

The Marxist heresy is another case in point. Its materialism is notorious. The baneful consequence of its projected millenium is ironically the worst hell of tyranny which men have ever invented. Yet this same Marxism taught us to view the social and economic tensions of society with more realism than ever before. We can appreciate the truth of its analyses, even if we now know that its conception of the "class structure" of society is too simple and that its view of the "class struggle" obscures all the mutualities which transcend the social tensions. We need the modicum of truth in even the Marxist as in the Freudian error, if we are to know the full truth about man.

On a much higher level, are all the disciplines of the "enlightenment" of philosophy, sociology and political science which survey the human scene. At worst they obscure the human self in its dignity and misery, living under the illusion that selves are merely minds. But at best, they offer many valid insights about the life of man in history, about the consequence of certain policies in economic and political life, about the common elements in certain historic phenomena, and about the variety and the uniformity of human behavior in this strange drama of human history.

We must add to the disciplines, which are most likely to be infected with "heresy" from the Christian standpoint, those disciplines, like historiography, history of literature, and of art (and, in fact, of all the traditional historical disciplines) which established their standards before modern heresies infected the study of man, and which are too close to the drama of human events and too conscious of its dramatic unpredictabilities to give themselves to the illusion that man is either pure mind or mere animal. If we add these disciplines, we must realize that the whole project of "freeing" the mind by rational disciplines is a very creative one and must be pursued in freedom, even if that freedom holds the possibility of periodically generating errors.

If we are sure enough of the truth which we hold as religious people, we will not be too anxious that what is false in these disciplines, will ever permanently obscure the truth about man and God which we have seen. This is the more true in our own day in which the rationalistic and naturalistic illusions are being dispelled; and the truth is again coming into view. The path of truth has been a tortuous and circuitous one. But it has come through the journey of the past centuries enriched by this encounter with its "enemies," and also purged of many aberrations which were the consequence of human folly seeking its last hiding place in the sanctuary of God. Therefore we have no reason to despair of either the commitments of faith or of the freedom of the mind, which are logically incompatible, but both of which are necessary for a wholesome life.

The reason for this relationship between religion and a free mind can be briefly summarized: a) The self is not identical with its mind. b) The mind may enrich the self, but it can not free the self from its interests. c) The self is emancipated from itself by its faith and trust beyond itself, but these commitments bind the mind as surely as the self's interest bind it. d) The worship of idols in modern political religions are more binding to the self and to the mind than mild forms of egocentricity, and the fact that these religions should have arisen in a period of "enlightenment" is proof that the relation between the self and its mind is more complicated than a culture with rationalistic illusions could realize. e) Even the worship of the true God who convicts all historic interests of their parochialism is no guarantee against restrictions upon the mind, for these partial and parochial interests participate in the ultimate religious commitment by becoming identified with the divine. f) This tendency to corruption and pretension in religion makes freedom of religion necessary in order that no religious community may have a monopoly of power and remain unchallenged by other faiths. Such freedom is necessary in order to preserve tolerable community under conditions of religious heterogeneity; but it is even more necessary to purify the various faiths. g) The freedom of the mind in a society has its own justification, because of the enrichment of life through the disciplines of culture which freedom makes possible. It has its special justification in relation to religion because the free mind, while less potent in delivering the self from its self-concern, is nevertheless able, not only to enrich the self, but provisionally to free the self from too narrow concerns and divert its interests to the larger world. Furthermore the rational analysis of all the coherences and sequences of life and history is an antidote against the cultural obscurantism into which the disciplines of faith periodically fall because they avail themselves of poetic, rather than scientific, ways of knowing. This freedom is necessary even though it is apparent that the disciplines which avail themselves of it usually propagate either one of two heresies: 1) that the self and the mind are identical and that God is identical with the rational order of the world, and 2) that the self is not significantly different from the brutes of nature and that it does not have the freedom which is the basis of all its religious striving. These heresies must be tolerated for the modicum of truth which emerges from the labors of these disciplines of culture.